# THE ULTIMATE Wreath BOOK

Hundreds of Beautiful Wreaths
to Make from
Natural Materials

## ELLEN SPECTOR PLATT

Rodale Press, Inc.
Emmaus, Pennsylvania

The author and editors who compiled this book have tried to make all of the contents as accurate and as cor-rect as possible. Illustrations, photographs, and text have all been carefully checked and cross-checked. However, due to the variability of materials, personal skill, and so on, neither the author nor Rodale Press assumes any re-sponsibility for any injuries suffered or for damages or other losses incurred that result from the material pre-sented herein. All instructions should be carefully studied and clearly understood before beginning a project.

The author and editors at Rodale Press hope you will join with us in preserving nature's beauty so that others may share in the enjoyment of nature crafting. Unless you are certain that the plants or plant materials you are collecting—including leaves, stems, bark, flowers, fruits, seeds, or roots—are very common in your area, or over a wide geographic area, please do not collect them. Do not disturb or collect any plants or plant materials from parks, natural areas, or private lands without the permis-sion of the owner. To the best of our knowledge, the plants and plant materials recommended in this book are common natural materials that can be grown and col-lected without harm to the environment.

**Photo Credits**

*Photo page viii, top:* The Metropolitan Museum of Art, Purchase, Joseph Pulitzer Bequest, 1938. (38.11.12) All rights reserved, The Metropolitan Museum of Art.

*Photo page viii, bottom:* The Metropolitan Museum of Art, Purchase, The Annenberg Foundation Gift, 1990. (1990.53.2) Copyright © 1990 by The Metropolitan Museum of Art.

*Photo page ix, top:* Philadelphia Museum of Art: W. P. Wilstach Collection.

*Photo page ix, bottom:* The Metropolitan Museum of Art, Purchase, Joseph Pulitzer Bequest, 1921. (21.116) Photograph by Schecter Lee. Copyright © 1986 by The Metropolitan Museum of Art.

*Photo page 5:* The book shown in the photo is used by permission of Riverside Book Co., Inc.

## The Ultimate Wreath Book Editorial Staff

**Editor:** Cheryl Winters Tetreau
**Cover and Book Designer:** Patricia Field
**Illustrator:** Emilie Snyder
**Photographer:** Mitch Mandel
**Photographer's Assistant:** Troy Schnyder
**Senior Researcher:** Heidi Stonehill
**Studio Manager:** Leslie Keefe
**Copy Editor:** Maria Kasprenski Zator
**Photo Stylist:** Ellen Spector Platt
**Assistant Stylist:** Toni Groff
**Manufacturing Coordinator:** Melinda B. Rizzo
**Editorial Assistance:** Stephanie Wenner

## Rodale Books

**Editorial Director, Home and Garden:**
 Margaret Lydic Balitas
**Senior Editor, Craft Books:**
 Cheryl Winters Tetreau
**Art Director, Home and Garden:**
 Michael Mandarano
**Copy Director, Home and Garden:**
 Dolores Plikaitis
**Office Manager, Home and Garden:**
 Karen Earl-Braymer
**Editor-in-Chief:**
 William Gottlieb

If you have any questions or comments concerning this book, please write to:

 Rodale Press, Inc.
 Book Readers' Service
 33 East Minor Street
 Emmaus, PA 18098

Printed in the United States of America on acid-free ∞ paper

## Library of Congress Cataloging-in-Publication Data
Platt, Ellen Spector
  The ultimate wreath book : hundreds of beautiful wreaths to make from natural materials / Ellen Spector Platt
    p.  cm.
    ISBN 0–87596–720–5 (hardcover : alk. paper)
    1. Wreaths. 2. Nature craft. I. Title.
TT899.75.P53  1995
745.92'6—dc20                                   95–22132

**Distributed in the book trade by St. Martin's Press**

2  4  6  8  10  9  7  5  3  1    hardcover

*To the best my garden grew:*
*David, Michael, and Jenny*

# contents

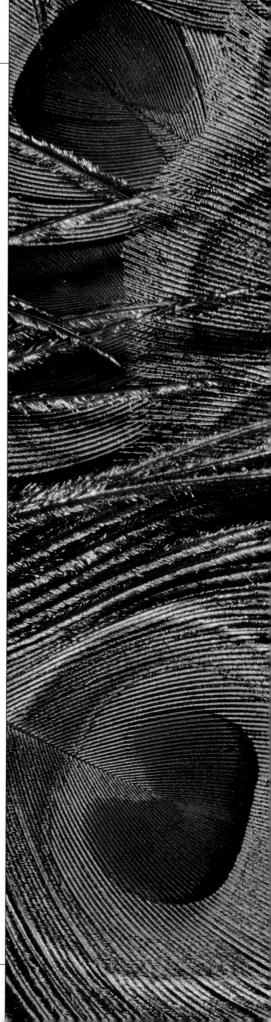

## Chapter 4: Theme Wreaths

## Chapter 5: Holiday Wreaths

## CHAPTER 6: WREATHS IN A RAINBOW OF COLORS

## CHAPTER 7: WREATHS IN ALL SIZES

## CHAPTER 8: SHAPES AND MATERIALS

## CHAPTER 9: THE BASICS

# Introduction

The goal I set in this, my third book of flowers and herbs, was to design 150 wreaths, dried and fresh, tiny and huge, blazing with color and subtly shaded. I wanted shapes that were unusual, themes that were both personal and universal, and natural materials that would demand you to take a second look. Above all, I wanted you to look through the book and think, *I'd love to make that, and I think I can.*

Over the years I've taught a variety of subjects to a varied audience: nature groups in day camp; Girl Scout and Cub Scout groups; college students; mentally disabled people; and executives, foremen, and factory workers. I'm still teaching in my late-blooming career of flower and herb farming. I find that girls who are dragged to demonstrations by their mothers rush home to try their first arrangement. Adults who come to a class thinking they're too inexperienced and not "crafty" or creative usually leave astonished that they were able to produce a pleasing design.

Friends who heard of my plan for this book made helpful suggestions for unusual wreaths: a soup wreath featuring dried vegetables and herbs—when you're tired of it, throw it in the pot and serve it up for dinner. Or how about a sausage wreath that winds fat links around a large ring bologna with a few onions, potatoes, and dried peppers for decoration—when you get tired of the wreath, throw it in the pot for dinner!

One of my favorite suggestions, the fruit of a hilarious session by the book's creative team, is pictured on the left. On the last day of photography, I served the "Bagel Wreath" to an appreciative audience of Mitch Mandel (Photographer), Trish Field (Book Designer), Troy Schnyder (Photographer's Assistant), and Toni Groff (Assistant Stylist). An "after" photo would have shown little more than a few crumbs and some smears of cream cheese after we made short work of this wreath. I've promised a reappearance of the "Bagel Wreath" to Cheryl Winters Tetreau, my delightful editor who was unable to partake of the original.

In preparation for writing this book, I went on scavenger hunts in two great art museums within driving

Right: *From Antioch, Roman Villa at Daphne,*
Mosaic Pavement: Central Panel
Personification of Spring

distance of my home, the Philadelphia Museum of Art and New York City's Metropolitan Museum of Art. Searching for wreath motifs in paintings, sculptures, and the decorative arts, I scoured art books for similar ideas. I was aided by discussions with and materials lent by art historian Debra Taylor Cashion, Ph.D., and medieval historian Ruth Mazo Karras, Ph.D.

While many Americans associate wreaths with Christian symbolism, earlier times and other cultures also adopted circles, rings, and wreaths to represent life, regeneration, birth, and fertility as well as death, mourning, and sacrifice. Wreaths can also signify glory, victory, and happiness. The meanings are ambivalent, and as with other symbols, they have changed through the ages and with different cultures.

In Greek and Roman times, the laurel or olive wreath signified wisdom. Starting in the seventh century B.C., laurel wreaths were bestowed on the winners of contests for music, poetry, and athletics in the Panhellenic games. Laurel was sacred to Apollo, the god of the muses. Olive wreaths were awarded at the Olympic games, and ivy wreaths were awarded for drama. Roman emperors wore wreaths of roses. We still speak of "heaping laurels" upon a person in recognition of achievement.

Once I started looking, the wreath motif popped up everywhere. From regal crowns to graceful hair garlands, from incised decoration on a sixteenth century Chinese silver cup stand to an eighteenth century Ottoman cradle inlaid with flowery wreath ornamentation made of mother-of-pearl. However, the use of head wreaths and garlands by women was preached against in the Middle Ages. A fourteenth century Dominican friar in England exhorted against women who wore wreaths or garlands to ornament their heads, claiming it led men to lust and the fires of Hell.

In the Christian prayer book of Michelino da Besozzo, a lovely and delicately illustrated manuscript from the early 1400s, both the prayers

Below: *Pietro Bernini,*
Herm of Priapus

Above: *Frans Snyders,*
Garland with Bust of Ceres

Below: *Andrea della Robbia,*
Prudence

themselves and the illustrations on the facing pages are wreathed with the brilliant beauty of small flowers supported by golden trellises. Each flower illustrating the manuscript was chosen for its symbolism. Long before the Victorians popularized the language of flowers, da Besozzo chose violets, pea and bean blossoms, borage, and cornflowers—among other less recognizable botanicals—to symbolize qualities such as healing and humility.

In Sandro Botticelli's magnificent painting *Primavera (Spring),* commissioned by the Medici family and painted in 1477–1478, flowers abound. Spring herself, displayed in a field of flowers under an orange grove, wears a dress adorned with fresh blossoms and a head crown and neck wreath of flowers and leaves, her waist encircled by another garland while she tosses flowers as she moves. The many interpretations of this painting place the goddess of spring as the creative force of nature.

In the late 1400s and early 1500s, Andrea della Robbia fashioned wreaths of fruits, flowers, cones, and leaves in white-glazed clay that surrounded a clay portrait or a coat of arms. This is one of the first examples I found of wreaths hanging on a wall, used as sumptuous room decoration, rather than being worn.

In the present, wreaths are popular decorative elements used to express welcome throughout North America. Hung on front doors and all through the house, they come in every conceivable size, shape, color, and material. As you use this book to make a wreath, know that you are part of a tradition that goes back more than 2,500 years.

Throughout this book, I have made every attempt to give specific and clear project instructions. Many people will automatically substitute the materials listed with materials they have available or those they like better. I'm delighted that they do. Where exact amounts are not listed, more of this or less of that is totally dependent on what *you* have on hand, and this will make the wreath your own creation. In Chapter 9, "The Basics," there is a section on designing your own wreath that explores different ways you can treat familiar materials. Above all, let your mind wander freely into the land of imagination. And enjoy your walk for what it is—all yours.

*Ellen Spector Platt*

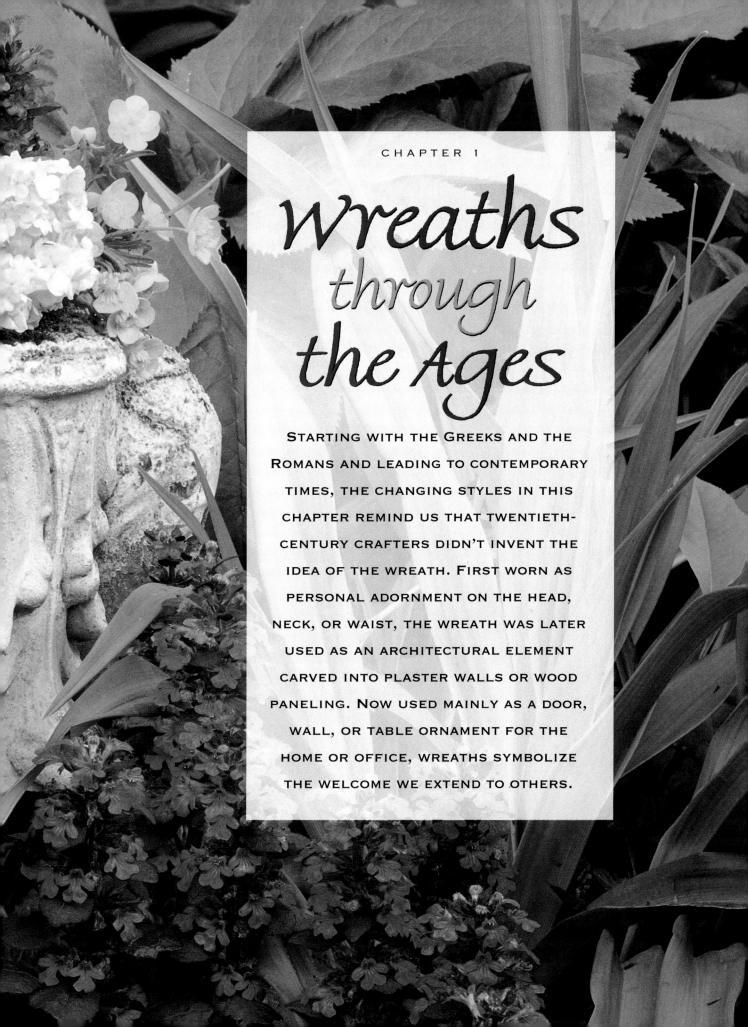

# CHAPTER 1

# Wreaths
## *through*
## *the Ages*

STARTING WITH THE GREEKS AND THE
ROMANS AND LEADING TO CONTEMPORARY
TIMES, THE CHANGING STYLES IN THIS
CHAPTER REMIND US THAT TWENTIETH-
CENTURY CRAFTERS DIDN'T INVENT THE
IDEA OF THE WREATH. FIRST WORN AS
PERSONAL ADORNMENT ON THE HEAD,
NECK, OR WAIST, THE WREATH WAS LATER
USED AS AN ARCHITECTURAL ELEMENT
CARVED INTO PLASTER WALLS OR WOOD
PANELING. NOW USED MAINLY AS A DOOR,
WALL, OR TABLE ORNAMENT FOR THE
HOME OR OFFICE, WREATHS SYMBOLIZE
THE WELCOME WE EXTEND TO OTHERS.

# Don't Rest on Your Laurels

*In* Greek and Roman times, a wreath on the head symbolized honor, and a laurel wreath was presented in honor of special achievement. Here is a simple wreath to award to the winner of a competition or to use to decorate a statue or doll.

## what You Need

10 to 12 stems of dried laurel or pre-
    served olive, or a combination of both
Assortment of small dried flowers
    (optional)
Heavy wire, like 18-gauge wire
Floral tape
Floral spool wire
Clippers
Wire cutters
Hot glue gun and glue sticks (optional)

## what You Do

1. Cut the heavy wire to fit the head size, taking into account the opening in the front. Wrap it with floral tape. Then bend the covered wire to form the head wreath.

2. Cut the laurel or olive stems into pieces about 5 inches long. Starting at one end of the covered wire wreath, lay two pieces along the wreath and wrap the stems to the wreath with the spool wire. Then add another two stems and wrap. Continue adding stems and stop at the middle of the wreath.

3. Start at the other end of the wreath and wrap in the same way. Meet in the middle and hide any wire with smaller bits of laurel or olive.

4. This wreath is traditionally made of leaves only, but you can add colored decoration by hot-gluing on dried flowers, if desired.

# Della Robbia Wreath

*I*n New York City's Metropolitan Museum of Art hang two wreaths by the Italian artist Andrea della Robbia (1435–1525). Made of white-glazed clay, they are a lush blend of pears, lemons, grapes, cucumbers, and leaves. This wreath, of real fruit and leaves, is reminiscent of the della Robbia style.

## *What You Need*

Assortment of whole dried fruits, vegetables, and leaves (Here I used 4 artichokes, 2 pink grapefruits, 11 limes, 10 pomegranates, 6 lemons, 7 oranges, and 15 lemonleaf [salal] leaves. See "Wreathmaker's Wisdom" on page 4.)

14-inch-diameter straw wreath base
18-inch square of green sheet moss
Floral spool wire
6 to 10 pieces of 18-inch-long green floral wire
Clippers
Wire cutters
Hot glue gun and glue sticks

## *What You Do*

1. Cover the wreath base with the sheet moss and wrap securely in place with the spool wire. As you work, cut and piece the moss as necessary to cover the front and sides of the wreath.

2. Using the green floral wire, wire the large vegetables and fruits through their bases. Attach the artichokes to the wreath base first. Place one on the wreath and wrap the wire around the wreath. Twist the wire tightly on the back of the wreath and cut off any excess wire. Place the other three artichokes evenly around the wreath.

3. Place the two grapefruits at the bottom of the wreath and secure in the same manner. Then wire the other fruits onto the wreath. Glue the smallest fruits on top of some of the other fruits. This wreath started out to be very even, but since the fruits are not all the same size, problems soon developed. Aim for visual balance—what fruits and vegetables look to be the same weight—rather than equality in numbers.

4. Tuck in the lemonleaf (salal) foliage around the wreath and glue in place.

## WREATHMAKER'S ❧WISDOM❧

*It's not difficult to dry whole citrus fruits. Follow these steps. Select sound fruit that feels solid but not overly juicy rather than the best citrus for eating. With a sharp knife, slice through the rind and barely cut into the flesh. Make five to eight cuts, from top to bottom, depending on the size of the fruit (make more cuts in larger fruit). Stop just short of the top and bottom points so you don't slice completely through the citrus. Place the cut fruit on a screen or cookie rack in a very warm, dark, dry place.*

*For the larger fruit, slip a piece of floral wire through the fruit 1½ inches up from the bottom. Allow the fruit to dry completely with the wire in place.*

*It will take about two to four weeks for the fruit to dry completely. The drying time will be determined by the size and juiciness of the fruit, and the temperature and humidity surrounding the drying screen. Dried fruit will feel very light.*

*To dry the artichokes, look for a large size and fresh, green color. Slip a piece of floral wire through the base of the choke and allow to dry as above.*

*Small pomegranates are hard to find in the market because they don't make good eating fruit. Purchase small, already-dried pomegranates from a floral or craft supply store.*

# Renaissance Faire

Botticelli's *Primavera* shows the goddess of spring enwreathed with flowers. Fresh flowers were often woven into the hair as adornment. Fashion this simple head wreath for a prom-goer or a bride.

## What You Need

Assortment of fresh flowers, herbs, and foliage (Here I used 2 stems of lavender lisianthus, 2 stems of boxwood, 1 stem of green lavender cotton, 7 bachelor's-buttons, 4 marigolds, 6 verbena flowers, and 5 stems of ageratum.)

2 yards of twisted paper ribbon

Clippers

Low-temperature glue gun and glue sticks, or Oasis floral glue

## What You Do

1. Using the entire length of paper ribbon (do not untwist), make a circle that is 1 inch larger in diameter than the size you need to fit the appropriate head. (This head wreath is 8 inches in diameter, so I made a 9-inch-diameter circle.) Weave the extra length under and over and between the paper ribbon.

The circle will hold without any additional fastening and gets a little smaller as you weave.

2. Cut all the flower stems off, reserving all the flowers and buds. Cut the boxwood and green lavender cotton into 3- to 4-inch pieces.

3. Glue the flowers, herbs, and foliage to the outside of the ring, starting with the largest materials first and then adding the smaller flowers, foliage, and buds.

### ELLEN'S EXTRAS

THE FRESH HEAD WREATH, SHOWN IN THE PHOTO ABOVE, LOOKED WONDERFUL EVEN AFTER 24 HOURS, THOUGH IT HAD BEEN LEFT AT ROOM TEMPERATURE. AFTER 48 HOURS, THE VERBENA WAS THE FIRST TO WILT, BUT THE OTHER FLOWERS WERE STILL VIBRANT. TRY WORKING WITH THOSE FLOWERS, SUCH AS CARNATIONS, ALSTROEMERIA, SMALL ORCHIDS, AND SMALL MUMS, THAT ARE TYPICALLY USED IN CORSAGES BECAUSE THEY HOLD UP WELL OUT OF WATER.

# A Colonial-American Preserved Wreath

*F*ollow the symmetrical, simple style of colonial decorations to create a wreath that will last for several years. (Although we photographed this wreath on a wrought iron gate, it should be protected from the elements.)

## What You Need

50 to 55 preserved magnolia leaves
6 dried pomegranates
11 or 12 halves of dried milkweed pods, cleaned of seeds
16 dried yarrow heads
12 to 14 dried strawflower heads
12-inch-diameter straw wreath base
Floral pins
Clippers
Hot glue gun and glue sticks

## What You Do

1. Pin the magnolia leaves dull side up on the wreath base, with the leaf tips pointing outward. Use two floral pins per leaf.

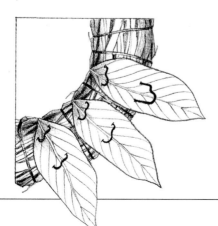

2. Turn the wreath over to what is now the "good" side. The leaves you have already pinned form a halo around the outside of the wreath. Now pin more magnolia leaves to the face of the wreath. Pin them in a circle, overlapping the leaves as you go in order to hide the pin of the previous leaf.

3. Glue the pomegranates around the wreath, evenly spaced at the 2, 4, 6, 8, 10, and 12 o'clock positions. Now glue the milkweed pods, interior side showing, around the top and bottom pomegranates. Here I have four on the top and seven on the bottom. Make your own favorite arrangement. Glue on the yarrow and strawflower heads last.

# A Boxwood Welcome

*I*n Virginia's Colonial Williamsburg, boxwood hedges ring many of the gardens. Snippets of boxwood find their way into many of the natural decorations adorning the homes and shops. Colonial-American wreaths included the use of fresh fruits—those that grew locally—or, for wealthier people, those that were imported. Placement of the materials was highly organized and symmetrical.

## What You Need

125 to 150 stems of boxwood, each 8 to 10 inches long (Or you can substitute other greens that you have available.)

18-inch-diameter wire box frame (The finished wreath is 28 inches in diameter.)

3 large lemons and 3 small lemons, fresh

4 fresh tangerines

4 fresh apples

8 pinecones or other cones

24 stems of dried white berries, like tallow or bayberries

14 Japanese lantern pods, or other small fresh fruit or pods (optional)

1 small bottle of whole cloves (optional)

Floral spool wire

Nail or toothpick

14 pieces of 18-inch-long green floral wire

14 floral picks

Clippers

Wire cutters

Hot glue gun and glue sticks

## What You Do

1. Buy or make the boxwood wreath base. (See "Wire Box Frame" on page 237 for instructions.)

### ELLEN'S EXTRAS

THIS WREATH CAN BE HUNG OUTDOORS EVEN IN FREEZING TEMPERATURES AND WILL LAST ONE MONTH OR MORE. WARM TEMPERATURES ARE MORE OF A PROBLEM THAN COLD BECAUSE THE FRUIT WILL ROT AND NEED REPLACING. TO MAKE THE MOST OF YOUR WREATH, START WITH FRUIT THAT IS UNDERRIPE AND USE NOTHING THAT IS SOFT OR BLEMISHED.

2. Decorate the lemons with cloves, if desired, by punching a small hole through the lemon skin with the nail or toothpick and inserting a clove. Decorate the lemons in different patterns, as shown in the photo on the opposite page, or all in the same pattern. You don't have to cover the whole lemon to get the effect.

3. Pierce each lemon, tangerine, and apple all the way through from side to side with a piece of 16-gauge wire. Then bend the wire across the back of the fruit.

4. Wrap the pinecones to floral picks. Then make six bundles of berries with four stems per bundle. Wrap the bundles to floral picks.

5. Place each piece of fruit where you want it on the boxwood wreath base. Stick the wires through to the back of the wreath and twist them together securely. Either cut off the wire ends or carefully bend them back to be out of the way.

6. When all the fruit is wired on, insert the cones and berries on picks into the thickness of the boxwood. Glue the Japanese lanterns to the boxwood, if desired.

# colonial-Style Door Wreath

*F*resh fruits and greens enhance the rich textures of dried cones and pods. In keeping with true colonial style, use mostly local material (here everything but the kumquats) and no ribbon to retain the natural feel.

## What You Need

24 long, thin cones, like white-pine cones
23 dried, thin pods, like catalpa
11 slices of dried osage-orange
11 or 12 sprigs of fresh evergreens, like pine
Fresh kumquats
Fresh crabapples
12-inch-diameter wire box frame (The finished wreath is 24 inches in diameter.)
Bucket of hot water
Spray shellac, varnish, or polyurethane (optional)
Floral spool wire
Floral wire (optional)
Clippers
Wire cutters
Hot glue gun and glue sticks

## What You Do

1. Soak the cones in hot water for about 30 minutes. They will close their "petals." Drain.

2. The cones will probably be of different lengths. With the clippers, cut off the bottoms of any overly long cones until they are about 6½ inches long. Insert the cones in the wreath frame, sliding them under the middle two wires, as shown in the illustration on the right. This task takes some time. If they won't

push straight in, you may have to wiggle them from side to side as you push them into place. Make sure about half the length of the cone extends out from the frame.

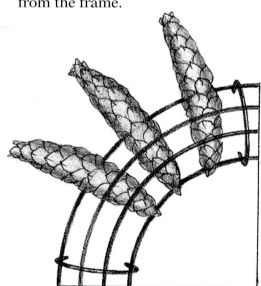

3. Insert the catalpa pods into the wreath frame, between the cones, in the same way. Put the wreath in a warm place to allow the cones to fully dry and reopen. It will take about five days.

4. Glue the osage-orange slices onto the cones in an overlapping circle. Spray with shellac, varnish, or polyurethane, if desired, to make the dried material more impervious to the weather.

5. Tuck the greens in the spaces between the cones. Add glue for reinforcement.

6. Glue the kumquats and the crabapples to the cones, going around the wreath in a pleasing pattern. If you feel the glue will not be secure enough, you can use pieces of green floral wire to wire on each piece of fruit. (See "Wreathmaker's Wisdom" on page 4 for instructions on wiring fruit.)

## ELLEN'S EXTRAS

THE DRIED MATERIALS ON THIS WREATH WILL LAST FOR YEARS. BEFORE STORING THE WREATH, REMOVE THE FRESH FRUIT AND GREENS. NEXT YEAR REDECORATE IN ANY WAY YOU CHOOSE.

# Victorian Wreath

The Victorian style of decorating was highly embellished and abundant, often overflowing with a romantic feel. Family photos in ornate frames were part of the decor. Because glass frequently doesn't survive over the years, frames sold without glass can be purchased at bargain prices.

## What You Need

Assortment of dried flowers and herbs
(Here I used 10 stems of lamb's-ear, 30 stems of catmint, and 8 stems of strawflowers.)
Old oval frame without glass (Here it is 12 x 16½ inches.)
2 yards of 2-inch-wide wire-edged ribbon
2 yards of ½-inch-wide wire-edged ribbon
Floral spool wire
14-inch-long thin, but rigid, straight stick (Here I used a hyacinth stake.)
Clippers
Scissors
Wire cutters
Hot glue gun and glue sticks

## What You Do

1. Wrap the oval frame with the 2-inch-wide ribbon, allowing some of the frame to show. Glue the ribbon at the start and finish, and trim off the excess.

2. Wrap the ½-inch-wide ribbon on top of the first, winding it around the frame. Glue at the start and finish.

3. Divide the flowers and herbs into two equal piles, intermingling the materials. Each pile should be about 10 inches long; trim the stems as necessary.

4. Wrap each pile with the spool wire to hold it. Now lay the bundles stem to stem, with the stems of one bundle overlapping the other. Slip the stick underneath the bundles and bind them all together with the spool wire to make a swag.

5. Wrap the middle of the swag with the 2-inch-wide ribbon and glue it in place. Then tie the ½-inch-wide ribbon around the middle of the wider ribbon and make a simple bow.

6. Place the swag across the frame until you are satisfied with the angle. Trim the stick so it will just rest on the frame but not be visible. Glue the ends of the stick directly to the oval frame.

# Victorian Arch

*I*n the center square of my town sits a late-Victorian home, lovingly restored by the young couple who bought this "white elephant." Fortunately, the tin-covered walls and lovely oak woodwork remain intact. I made this flowered arch to reflect the ornate qualities of the arches that grace the area between their dining room and parlor.

## What You Need

Assortment of dried flowers (Here I used 3 stems of blue hydrangea, 6 dahlias, 9 cockscomb, 13 roses, 10 strawflowers, and 15 lamb's-ear leaves.)
Briar arch wreath base
Two 2-yard lengths of ivory or ecru lace
Clippers
Hot glue gun and glue sticks

## What You Do

1. Make the briar arch wreath base. (See "Briar Arch and Sorghum Swirl" on page 214 for instructions.)

2. Take one piece of lace and loosely drape it under and over the frame of the wreath base, sticking it to the briar thorns and dabbing glue to hold it where necessary. Leave some slack as you do this to form small loops or swirls. Take the other piece of lace and do the same, filling in where there are spaces.

### ELLEN'S EXTRAS

WHEN MAKING THIS ARCH WREATH, SUBSTITUTE FLOWERS FREELY ACCORDING TO WHAT YOU HAVE AVAILABLE. WHEN MAKING ANY VICTORIAN-STYLE WREATH, YOU HAVE AN OPPORTUNITY TO USE SOME FADED FLOWERS. HERE THE ROSES, KEPT FOR SEVERAL YEARS IN A PLASTIC BAG, LOST MOST OF THEIR COLOR BUT NOT THEIR STRUCTURE, AND SEEMED PERFECT FOR THIS "ANTIQUE" DESIGN. I CHOSE COCKSCOMB AND STRAWFLOWERS IN A PALE SHADE, ALSO GIVING THE IMPRESSION OF AGE.

3. Cut all the flower stems short. Break the hydrangea heads into pieces. Glue on a large piece at the bottom center, then glue pieces at the bottom ends and at the top center. Fill in the bare spots with whatever hydrangea pieces you have left.

4. Glue on the other flowers according to size, with the largest first (here the dahlias and cockscomb) and ending with the roses, strawflowers, and lamb's-ear leaves.

# A Wreath in the Style of Josiah Wedgwood

Josiah Wedgwood designed jasperware, often decorated with wreaths and swags of fruits, flowers, and leaves. I've tried to capture that Wedgwood look in a wreath that complements the genuine jasperware.

## What You Need

Assortment of dried flowers, grasses, and pods (Here I used 6 Japanese lantern pods, 12 oriental nigella pods, 24 small pieces of German statice, 12 stems of peppergrass, and 18 individual pods cut from 3 stems of pennycress.)

2 extruded foam wreath bases, each 14 inches in diameter

Gesso (optional)

Wedgwood blue spray paint

White enamel spray paint

Spray lacquer

Clippers

Craft glue

Hot glue gun and glue sticks

Paintbrush

## What You Do

1. With the craft glue, glue the two wreath bases together, one on top of the other, and let dry. (Hot glue tends to melt foam, but it is fine for gluing on the flowers.)

2. If desired, brush the front and sides of the wreath with the gesso to smooth out the texture of the foam. I wanted the wreath to look less like colored foam and more like porcelain, so I used three coats here and let it dry between coats. You can buy gesso at an art supply store.

3. When the gesso is dry, spray the wreath blue. Spray the flowers with one to three coats of white enamel paint to cover and give a nice sheen. If you stand the flowers in an old can while spraying, it makes this step a little easier.

4. Clip the stems of the flowers and pods as short as needed and glue onto the wreath in a regular pattern. Then spray the entire wreath with lacquer to give it additional sheen.

# Contemporary Flair

*W*ander through a hardware store, an office supply store, or a sewing shop and discover materials that are just begging to be used for craft designs. When I went to my local hardware store and asked for 8 feet of copper refrigerator tubing, the owner inquired if I knew how to do the job. I explained that for less than the cost of a good ribbon, copper tubing can serve the same purpose on a wreath. He just shook his head.

## What You Need

4 branches of fresh curly willow, each about 6 feet long (This is the size most florists have.)
1 bunch of 2-foot-tall dried pampas grass
32 inches of 16- or 18-gauge wire
24-gauge floral spool wire
8 feet of ¼-inch copper refrigerator tubing
12 inches of 20-gauge copper wire
Clippers
Wire cutters

## What You Do

1. Make a wire wreath frame by forming a circle with the 16- or 18-gauge wire and wrapping the ends around each other to secure.

2. Note that each branch of curly willow branches off into many thinner stems. Cut off the thick bottom part and discard, or use to root and start your own shrub. Cut the top into pieces approximately 2 feet long.

3. Tie the spool wire onto the frame. You will be wrapping the willow branches to the frame. (See "Single-Wire Frame" on page 235 for instructions.) Take two to four branches of willow and wrap them tightly to the frame with the spool wire. Continue all around the frame, wrapping on clusters of additional branches. When you are finished, tie off and cut the wire.

4. Roll the copper tubing into a tight spiral, about 4 inches in diameter. Then pull the two ends outward to make an open spiral. The narrow part of the spiral goes at the bottom and the more open part at the top. This serves as a container for the dried grasses. Tie the copper spiral to the wreath with small pieces of spool wire.

5. Tie the bunch of pampas grass near the bottom of the stems using the 20-gauge copper wire and insert it into the spiral.

# CHAPTER 2

# Dried and Fresh Floral Wreaths

THERE IS NO NEED TO BE CLEVER TO
ENHANCE THE BEAUTY OF A FLOWER—NO
NEED FOR ARTIFICE OR CUNNING. ALLOW
THE FLOWERS TO SPEAK FOR THEMSELVES,
AND YOU CAN'T GO WRONG. WITH DRIED
MATERIALS, LET COLOR AND TEXTURE
PREDOMINATE. WITH FRESH MATERIALS,
ALLOW COLOR AND FORM TO RULE. USE
FRESH AND DRIED FLOWERS IN QUANTITY
OR BY THE STEM—MASSING FLOWERS
CREATES SPECTACULAR RESULTS AND
EXAMINING THEM SINGLY REVEALS THE
WONDERFUL SECRETS OF THE UNIVERSE.

# A Very Pretty Wreath

*H*ow many times I've heard the disclaimer "I'm not creative" coming from novices in flower arranging! I tell students who worry not to strive for creativity—just to think of making something pretty or something they like. And, almost always, they are pleased with the results.

## What You Need

12 well-branched stems of dried 'Silver King' artemisia (more stems if they are not very full)

7 stems of dried blue delphinium or larkspur

7 air-dried wine-colored peonies

7 to 10 dried peach or pink roses and their leaves

10-inch-diameter straw wreath base

20 to 25 floral pins

Clippers

Hot glue gun and glue sticks

## What You Do

1. Cut the artemisia into 8- to 10-inch-long pieces. Pin them two-thirds of the way around the wreath base in clusters of four to five pieces, using the illustration as your guide. As you pin, angle each cluster outward, and pin the next cluster on top of the stems before.

2. Cut the delphinium stems 8 to 10 inches from the top. Reserve the bottom portion of the stems if they have blossoms on them. Intersperse the delphinium around the artemisia and glue it in place.

3. Take clusters of three to four artemisia stems and cover the rest of the wreath base, holding the artemisia in place with pins. On this third of the wreath, pin the artemisia only onto the surface of the base, not angling it outward.

4. Glue the peonies and then the roses to this last third of the wreath, as shown in the photo on the opposite page. Add the rose leaves and any individual delphinium blossoms that might have fallen in the construction process.

# Summer Meadow

*I* tried to achieve the feel of a stroll through the meadow with this combination of dried materials, though I've taken liberties. The buttercups are past blooming when the other meadow flowers burst forth, and the strawflowers replace scarlet field poppies, which don't dry well.

## What You Do

1. Buy or make the vine wreath base. (See "Woven Vine" or "Wrapped Vine" on page 234 for instructions.)

2. Make bundles of three to ten stems of buttercups and wrap with floral tape. Repeat this process with the bachelor's-buttons and the foxtail grass.

3. Glue on the background material first, starting with stems of goldenrod and black-eyed Susans. Next glue on small bundles of flowers, such as buttercups.

4. Finish the wreath by gluing on single stems, like strawflowers and fern leaves. Glue the Queen-Anne's-lace directly to the materials already in place.

## What You Need

Assortment of dried meadow flowers in any combination or quantity (Here I used buttercups; bachelor's-buttons; wild, green foxtail grass; goldenrod; black-eyed Susans; strawflowers; fern; and Queen-Anne's-lace.)

14- to 16-inch-diameter vine wreath base (Here I used wisteria.)

Floral tape

Clippers

Hot glue gun and glue sticks

### WREATHMAKER'S ❧ WISDOM ❦

*Here are the best methods for drying the materials used in this wreath:*

**Hang upside down:** *bachelor's-buttons, buttercups, foxtail grass, and goldenrod*

**Dry on a screen:** *Queen-Anne's-lace*

**Press:** *fern*

**Air-dry and wire the stems:** *strawflowers*

# Who's On First?

Let flowers pinch-hit for each other, rather than stick rigidly to the starting lineup. Sea lavender forms the airy base of this wreath; but you can substitute additional German statice, a botanical cousin. I recycled rose leaves from another project for the greenery.

## What You Need

10 stems of dried sea lavender

4 stems of dried German statice

Assortment of air-dried flowers and berries (Here I used 6 stems of coral bells, 3 stems of blue delphinium, 6 stems of pepperberries, 1 stem of yellow statice, 4 stems of love-in-a-mist, 6 stems of purple globe amaranth, and 18 rose leaves.)

7 pink dogwood blossoms dried in silica gel (optional)

16- or 18-gauge wire, 46 inches long

Floral spool wire

Clippers

Wire cutters

Hot glue gun and glue sticks

## What You Do

1. Make a 24-inch-diameter circle with the 16- or 18-gauge wire and twist the ends together to secure. Here I used 46 inches of wire to form the circle. (See "Single-Wire Frame" on page 235 for instructions.)

2. Cut the dried sea lavender into 6- to 9-inch-long pieces. Attach the lavender to the wire circle with the spool wire, making sure the wire base is completely covered.

3. Cut the other materials into short pieces and glue them to the sea lavender. Glue on the German statice around the edges, then the more colorful flowers, working with one variety at a time and gluing it evenly around the wreath before starting on the next. Glue on the dogwood last, if desired, making sure it is visible.

# Do You Like Butter?

**W**hen we were kids, we held buttercups under a person's chin. If a golden reflection appeared, that was a sure indication of a butter predilection. I still like butter, and especially buttercups, which bloom in drifts in my back meadow, providing me with a good excuse not to mow before summer.

## What You Need

Assortment of floral materials for each 2-inch-diameter wreath: 30 fresh buttercups; 2 stems of dried pearly everlasting; 4 florets of dried larkspur; and 4 small blue or purple dried flowers like bachelor's-button, ageratum, a piece of statice, or a mixture of these

18-inch square frame with no glass (Here I had the framer line the mat board with fabric, but you could use a plain, colored mat board or a textured one, like grass cloth.)

8 pieces of 18- or 20-gauge wire, each 3 inches long

24-gauge or finer floral spool wire

Clippers

Wire cutters

Hot glue gun and glue sticks

## What You Do

1. To make each wreath, form a piece of 3-inch wire into a circle and twist the ends together to secure. The circle should be about 2 inches in diameter.

2. Cut off a 15-inch piece of spool wire and tie it to the wire circle. Then cut the stems of the buttercups to 3 inches. Take five buttercups, place them along the circle at a slight angle, and wrap tightly with the spool wire. Trim off any excess stem lengths so the little wreath doesn't get too thick. Take another five buttercups and lay them on top of the stems of the first bunch. Tie them in place with the spool wire and trim the stems.

3. With four more clusters of five buttercups, you should be all the way around the ring. After wrapping the last buttercups, turn the wreath over, tie off, and trim the excess wire.

4. Repeat Steps 1 through 3 until you have made eight small buttercup wreaths. Leave the wreaths lying face up on top of your refrigerator or in another warm, dry spot. They will dry in about five days.

5. When the wreaths are completely dry, glue on the other little flower decorations. In the project shown in the photo, one larkspur stem provides all the needed florets.

6. Glue the little wreaths in a circle to the mat board.

# Larkspur Pinwheel

Combine flowers that have rigid stems, like larkspur, with less stiff flowers, like golden bright star. Combine lavender, white, pink, and yellow for a springtime effect.

## What You Need

A large quantity of dried flowers (Here I used lavender larkspur, rodanthe daisy, immortelle, pink larkspur, and golden bright star.)
Green sheet moss
12-inch-diameter straw or extruded foam wreath base
50 or more floral pins
Clippers
Hot glue gun and glue sticks

## What You Do

1. Pin the moss to the wreath base, covering the front and sides completely.

2. Pin bunches of six to eight stems of lavender larkspur straight out at the 3, 6, 9, and 12 o'clock positions. Use several pins to hold each bunch securely.

3. Between each of the 4 larkspur bunches, pin bunches of white flowers that are 10 to 12 inches long. Here I used 2 bunches of rodanthe daisies and 1 bunch of immortelle totaling about 20 stems in each quadrant. Next scatter 14 stems of pink larkspur around the wreath by carefully sliding them under the existing pins.

4. Trim the stems of the flowers if they intrude into the center of the wreath. You will now have a nice pinwheel effect, but the floral pins will be showing.

5. Pin the remaining variety of dried flowers in a circle around the center of the wreath, covering the pins of the other flowers. Here I used golden bright star. Pin small bunches on the wreath and hide the stems with another bunch of flowers. Cut the stems of the last bunch to 2 to 3 inches so you can slip them under the heads of the first flowers.

# The warmth of the sun

*W*e gravitate naturally to the light and warmth of the sun—and so do sunflowers. By adding the green of the hydrangeas and bay leaves to the golds and browns of the dried sunflowers, this wreath will look appropriate displayed all year. Forego the green, and you have a decoration strictly for fall.

## what You Need

5 sunflower pods in the seed stage

2 freeze-dried or silica-dried sunflowers

10 small air-dried sunflowers, heliopsis, and gloriosa daisies

9 small clumps of dried, greenish hydrangea

10 small clusters of dried bay leaves

2 vine wreath bases, each 16 inches in diameter (Here I used briar wreaths, but any thin vine will do.)

2 pieces of floral spool wire, each 10 inches long

Clippers

Wire cutters

Hot glue gun and glue sticks

## what You Do

1. Buy or make two vine wreath bases that are similar in size and shape. (See "Woven Vine" or "Wrapped Vine" on page 234 for instructions.)

2. Make a double wreath by wiring the two vine wreath bases together. Put one wreath on top of the other and wire the tops and bottoms together to form one wreath.

3. Glue the sunflower pods onto the vine, with one at the top, two on the bottom, and one on each side. Next glue on the two large sunflowers, then the smaller flowers and hydrangea stems. Lastly, fit in the bay leaves where you need a small, green accent. Note that although the pattern of the wreath is set in four sections, within each section the materials vary slightly in content and number, making a more interesting design.

# Hot-Pepper Topiary

Nothing but a wreath on a stick in a pot! Make a pair and graciously accept compliments.

## What You Need for Each Topiary

12-inch square of green sheet moss

Assortment of dried flowers and herbs (Here I used 9 globe centaurea and 8 oriental nigella pods for the edges; 4 lamb's-ears, 12 cayenne peppers, and 4 sprigs of bay leaf for each side; and several flowers and pods at the base.)

6-inch-diameter circle of corrugated cardboard, cut from a carton

Floral spool wire

1 cinnamon stick or other stick, 10 inches long

½ brick of brown floral foam or extruded foam

Clay flower pot, 4 to 6 inches in diameter

Clippers

Scissors

Wire cutters

Paring knife

Hot glue gun and glue sticks

## What You Do

1. Make the topiary form by cutting a 3-inch-diameter hole out of the center of the cardboard circle.

2. Wrap the cardboard form with sheet moss, saving some moss for the base of the pot. To hold the sheet moss in place, glue it down in several places and then wrap with the spool wire to secure.

3. With the spool wire, tie the top of the cinnamon stick to the mossy form. The form is now ready to decorate.

## ELLEN'S EXTRAS

YOU CAN USE THIS SAME TECHNIQUE TO MAKE VARIOUS SIZES OF TOPIARY WREATHS. SINCE YOU START WITH "FREE" MATERIAL—THE CORRUGATED CARDBOARD—AND CAN USE "FREE" STICKS FOR THE STEM, MAKE DRAMATIC YET INEXPENSIVE TOPIARIES FOR GRAND EVENTS BY DECORATING WITH APPROPRIATE COLORS AND MATERIALS. TO KEEP THE BASE SECURE FOR LARGE TOPIARIES, POUR PLASTER OF PARIS INTO A LINER POT THAT CAN BE PLACED INTO THE LARGER CLAY POT.

4. Glue the globe centaurea and nigella pods around the rim first; these flowers will be visible from both sides. Now glue the materials on the front, using the pattern shown in the photo or any other you desire. Gently turn the topiary over and glue down the materials for the reverse side, being careful not to crush your previous work.

5. Trim the floral foam with the paring knife to fit snugly into the flower pot, and jam it in the pot. With the clippers, cut the bottom of the cinnamon stick into a point and insert it in the middle of the pot. You only get one chance to do this because the foam will become too loose if you take out the stick and try to do it again. Use a different piece of foam to correct a problem.

6. Drape the moss over the foam and glue it in place. Glue on extra flowers at the base, if desired.

# The Party Table

Construct these leaf chargers and place card holders to go with the "Hot-Pepper Topiary" on page 34. Guests can take both of them home as a remembrance of your wonderful party.

## what you Need for a Leaf Charger

50 to 60 fresh leaves, like lamb's-ear or galax (available from florists)

12 to 15 dried cayenne peppers

Pieces of fresh or dried flowers and herbs in appropriate colors and styles, like bay leaves, lamb's-ear buds, oriental nigella pods, and purple statice

1 stiff paper plate, like Chinet, large enough to serve as an underplate (Here I used a 10-inch paper plate for use with an 8-inch dinner plate.)

Low-temperature glue gun and glue sticks, or thick white craft glue and toothpick

## what You Do

1. Glue the lamb's-ear or galax leaves onto the paper plate. They will dry in place. (Do not use a hot glue gun for this project because it may discolor the leaves. If you don't have a low-temperature glue gun, use craft glue.) Start on the outside rim of the plate and glue on the leaves in a ring, overlapping them by at least ½ inch. The leaves will shrink as they dry, and the paper plate will show through if you don't overlap generously. Keep gluing on leaves in concentric rings, getting closer and closer to the center until the plate is completely covered.

2. Glue the peppers and flowers to the outer rim in a repetitive pattern. The flowers and herbs used here can be dried or fresh; the fresh materials will dry in place. If you are using craft glue, apply it to the smaller flowers and herbs with the toothpick.

## what You Need for a Place Card Holder

5 pieces of stalk, each 4 inches long (Here I used sorghum, but you can use broomcorn or bamboo.)
3 or 4 dried cayenne peppers
3 or 4 nigella pods
1 stem of red pepperberries, 2 inches long
1 small name card
Clippers
Hot glue gun and glue sticks

## what You Do

1. Lay out four pieces of stalk, two on the bottom and two on the top, to form a square in the center. Glue down where they touch each other.

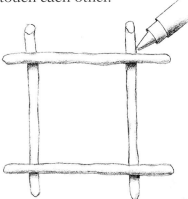

2. Decorate the square along two sides by gluing on the dried materials, starting with the peppers and then adding the nigella pods. Glue the stems of pepperberries onto the square.

3. Glue on the last piece of stalk to the top center at the back of the square to make a prop for the place card holder. Cut the stalk at an angle at the top and bottom to make the joint fit better and to make the stand more stable. With a tiny dab of glue, attach the name card to the holder.

# Radiant Wreath

*It's* low, lovely, and luminous. As a centerpiece, this wreath lasts for many months, awaiting a formal dinner party or a special dinner for two. Place it in the center of a dining table, away from constant jostling, to help ensure its longevity.

## What You Need

5 air-dried lemonleaf (salal) branches
10 silica-dried peonies
5 silica-dried roses
5 silica- or freeze-dried gardenias
10 silica-dried miniature daffodils
12-inch-diameter extruded foam ring
Sealing spray for dried flowers
1 pillar candle in a protective container
  (optional)
Clippers
Hot glue gun and glue sticks

## What You Do

1. Following the manufacturer's directions, spray the silica-dried flowers on all sides with the sealing spray. Set aside.

2. Cut the leaves off one branch of lemonleaf (salal). Glue the leaves around the inside of the ring, placing the leaves horizontally.

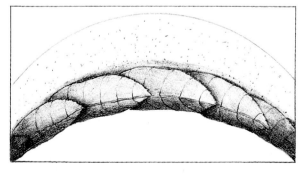

### Wreathmaker's Wisdom

*The materials in this design are dried in three ways. To achieve a look of perfection, dry your materials in silica gel. (See "Wreathmaking Necessities" on page 244 for information on silica gel.) Buy freeze-dried flowers, if desired, but you can get much the same effect with silica gel. Freeze-dried materials are heavily sprayed by the manufacturer with a protective spray. You must spray flowers dried in silica gel to prevent the reabsorption of humidity, and so prevent drooping. It is best to spray them before using in any arrangement.*

3. Cut 3- to 4-inch pieces of lemonleaf (salal) branches and insert them around the outside of the ring. Start with six pieces. You can always add more at the end to fill in if necessary.

4. Follow my usual principle of using the largest flowers first. Insert the dried peonies around the ring. If the stems are

very short, glue the peonies directly to the ring. Next add the roses and gardenias, either by inserting their stems into the foam or by gluing the flowers to the leaves.

5. Add more lemonleaf (salal) leaves between the flowers, both to fill in bare

spaces and to separate the colors. Add the miniature daffodils last for spots of vibrant color.

6. If you choose to use a candle in this centerpiece, be sure it is tall enough to clear the leaves and flowers. Remember never to leave a lit candle unattended.

# corrugated Table Topper

Make an inexpensive permanent wreath form to use as an unusual centerpiece or table topper. Change the materials with the seasons or to use at holiday times. It's a new idea for an old material.

## What You Need

Seasonal dried materials (Here, for fall, I used strawflowers, love-in-a-mist pods, wheat, protea pods, drumstick flower, globe thistle, Japanese lanterns, cockscomb, fern pods, oriental nigella, heliopsis, pepperberries, and cayenne peppers.)

18-inch and 20-inch squares of corrugated cardboard without the heavy backing used in cartons (save from packages you receive or buy at a packaging supply store)

14- to 16-inch-diameter mixing bowl

Floral tape

Green or brown floral foam (optional)

Small egg cup, votive holder, or other small "vase" (optional)

Clippers

Utility knife

Hot glue gun and glue sticks

Pencil

## What You Do

1. With the pencil, trace the rim of the mixing bowl onto the 18-inch square of corrugated cardboard. Using the knife, cut the circle from the cardboard.

2. From the 20-inch square of corrugated cardboard, cut a piece 4 inches wide and 20 inches long. Fold it in half the long way, with the ridges facing outward. (You can buy corrugated cardboard that is prescored for easy folding or make it easy yourself by scoring lightly on the reverse side of the fold with a small, sharp knifepoint.) Starting at one short end, roll the cardboard strip until you have a 2-inch-diameter tube and cut off the excess. Overlap the cut ends and glue them together.

3. Using what remains of the cardboard strip, continue to make other small tubes, some a little wider and some a little narrower. Make some of the tubes shorter by cutting a piece off the bottom of the cardboard before you glue it into the tube shape. Here I have 20 tubes of varying dimensions. When you run out of your first strip of cardboard, cut and fold another, then continue making as many tubes as you want.

4. Place a ring of tubes around the edge of the corrugated circle, filling in completely. Then add a few more on the interior of this ring. When you have the pattern set, glue each tube to the base.

5. Now for the fun part. Fill each tube with one kind of flower or pod. The narrower tubes may only hold one pod while others may hold a small bunch wrapped with floral tape to hold them together. If you want certain flowers to stand as upright as soldiers on parade, stuff the bottom of the tube with a small piece of floral foam, if desired.

6. As a final trim, glue one small pod, such as love-in-a-mist, around the outside between the tubes.

7. If desired, place a small "vase" in the center and fill it with one of the dried materials.

# Gourd Wreath

*T*his is a perfect wreath to hang in a sunny spot. Sunlight will bleach the neutral-color materials, resulting in a wreath that will look interesting for years.

## What You Need

21 small, dried gourds
21 stems of dried pampas grass
21 large, white dried strawflower heads
Assortment of other dried neutral flowers and pods (Here I used poppy pods; small, white strawflowers; bunny-tail; and quaking grass.)
18-inch-diameter straw wreath base
2 yards of decorative cording or ribbon
Clippers
Hot glue gun and glue sticks

## What You Do

1. Place the gourds around the wreath base to see how they will fit. Leave about 1 inch between them. Leave more space if you have fewer gourds. Glue them around the wreath, all facing the same way. Apply pressure to each gourd until the glue dries.

2. Next cut off the stems from the 21 stems of grass and glue the grass in place between the gourds. Glue the largest strawflowers between the gourds, alternating positions, as shown in the photo on the opposite page.

3. Glue on the rest of the dried materials, scattering them evenly between the gourds.

### WREATHMAKER'S WISDOM

*Living as I do in northeastern Pennsylvania—with our humid summers and damp, chilly winters—I find the process of drying gourds to be one of the mysteries of life. No matter what I do, some gourds will rot instead of dry. To increase my chances of success, I start with more than I think I need. I select sound gourds with no obvious blemishes that would start the rotting process. I then wash off all the dirt in detergent and water into which I splash some liquid bleach. I towel-dry the gourds and poke two holes in the sides where they may not be too obvious. Then I lay the gourds on a screen in an out-of-the-way place where it's warm and dry. Most will dry, but some won't. If you have a better method, call me.*

4. Loop the cording around the wreath, as shown in the photo on the opposite page, tucking the ends into the wreath. Glue it in several spots to secure.

# wreath in Bloom

*I*n the dead of winter, this blooming wreath will remind you that spring will actually appear. When narcissus bulbs are forced right in floral foam, you can place them in any design.

## What You Need

Forced narcissus bulbs in a floral foam "nest" (See "Wreathmaker's Wisdom" on this page.)
2 to 3 large handfuls of green sheet moss or Spanish moss
2 to 3 stems of pussy willow or bare twigs, each 14 to 16 inches long
1 large, dried sponge mushroom (optional)
12- to 14-inch-diameter vine wreath base
Floral spool wire
Floral pick (optional)
Bow (optional)
Clippers
Wire cutters

## What You Do

1. Buy or make a sturdy vine wreath base. (See "Woven Vine" or "Wrapped Vine" on page 234 for instructions.)

2. Wrap the sheet moss completely around the bulb nest. Secure the moss around the foam with spool wire.

3. Wire the covered nest to what will be the bottom of your wreath. To prevent the narcissus from flopping, insert several pieces of pussy willow through the moss into the foam. Use this to act as a trellis.

4. Tuck in other bits of sheet moss around the vine wreath base where there is space. If there is room, wire a large sponge mushroom to a floral pick and insert it into the foam. Add a bow to the side or top of the wreath, if desired.

5. Hang the wreath in a cool place, but don't allow the narcissus to freeze. Water carefully every few days.

## WREATHMAKER'S ❧ WISDOM ❧

*Fragrant paperwhite narcissus are the easiest bulbs to force. Purchase them in the fall and keep them in a cool place until six weeks before you want them to bloom.*

*To make a bulb nest, cut a brick of green floral foam in half. Soak the foam in water for 30 minutes. Use a tablespoon to scoop out round holes that are about 1 inch deep and 2 inches wide. Nestle each bulb in a hole. Each half-brick can hold three bulbs.*

*Set the nests in a shallow dish or pan of water in a cool, dark place for three weeks. Then bring the pan into the light for three weeks. Check frequently and add water as necessary. You will probably have blooms in six weeks.*

# It Might As Well Be Spring

With record-setting cold and snow outside the door, I forced forsythia and pussy willows to bloom inside. When winter starts to get you down, consider rushing spring with this fresh wreath.

## What You Need

10 to 12 branches of fresh pussy willow in bud, each 3 to 4 feet long

10 to 12 branches of fresh pussy willow in bud, each 2 feet long

6 to 8 branches of forsythia in bloom, each 1 to 2 feet long

1 handful of fresh or dried Spanish moss

Floral spool wire

Small Oasis Igloo

2 yards of ribbon (Here I used 2 yards each of gray and yellow ribbon; however, you can use just one color if you prefer.)

Clippers

Scissors

Wire cutters

## *What You Do*

1. Divide the longer pussy willow branches into two piles of about six branches each. Lay the piles on a table with the cut ends facing each other, then overlap the cut ends by 12 inches. The base of the wreath should be about 3 inches deep, giving you a fairly wide surface on which to attach the forsythia. Be sure to use only fresh pussy willow for this wreath. If the willow is dried out, it will break, not bend.

2. Unroll about 10 inches of spool wire for a "tail," then unroll more wire to bind the overlapped area of the pussy willow. Finish by leaving a second wire "tail" of about 10 inches. Secure the wire tails by weaving them under and over several of the previous turns. Cut off the excess wire and tuck the ends amid the branches.

3. Grasp the bud ends of the pussy willow bundle about 6 inches from the ends, with one end in each hand. Gently bring your hands together and cross the ends. Let the branch tips splay outward, as shown in the photo. Bind the branches with wire where they cross.

4. Take the shorter pussy willow branches and divide them into two equal piles. Wire each pile to the bottom of the wreath base with the tips at opposite ends and the branches overlapping.

> ## WREATHMAKER'S ❧ WISDOM ❦
>
> *Force both pussy willow and forsythia anytime after New Year's Day. Cut them and put them in warm water. Use fresh flower preservative according to the package directions, if desired. Allow two weeks for the blooms to appear, less as you get closer and closer to the natural bloom time or if the temperature has suddenly warmed, before you take cuttings.*

5. Soak the Oasis Igloo in water for 30 minutes. Remove and let drain. String wire through the two holes on either side of the Igloo and tie the Igloo securely to the bottom of the wreath. Drape with Spanish moss.

6. If you are cutting forsythia already in bloom, soak it in water eight hours or overnight. Insert the forsythia branches through the moss and into the Oasis Igloo. Make a bow with the ribbon and wire it to the top of the wreath where the branches cross. (See "Making a Bow" on page 243 for instructions.)

# Tulip Mania

*I*n the spring, I *have* to have masses of tulips to bring indoors. When you grow your own tulips, you can have an armload of color at a thrifty price. If cut while the buds start to show color and if they are properly conditioned, tulips last at least two weeks in water, less time in floral foam.

## What You Need

24 to 60 fresh tulips
10 fresh prunings from a shrub or tree, each 6 to 8 inches long (Here I used apple in bud.)
Fresh-flower food
Bucket of water
10- to 12-inch-diameter Oasis foam ring
Round platter or tray, 14 inches in diameter or more
Clippers

## What You Do

1. Add tepid water and flower food (dissolved according to the manufacturer's directions) to the bucket. The water should be high enough to come about one-third of the way up the flower stems.

### WREATHMAKER'S WISDOM

*If you grow your own tulips, fertilize the bulbs just after blooming and again in the fall, and they will rebloom for three to four years.*

*If you are buying cut tulips, look for leaves that are green and crisp, and flowers that are still green at the base. The bottom of the stems should be firm and not slimy. Tulip petals close up in the cold temperatures of a supermarket refrigerator, and customers can easily be fooled into thinking the flowers are fresh because they are closed.*

2. Remove any damaged leaves from the tulips. Recut the stems and stand the tulips in the bucket in a cool, dark place for at least eight hours to condition.

3. Soak the Oasis ring in a sink full of water for 30 minutes. Remove, drain, and wipe the bottom dry. Place on the platter or tray.

4. Recut the tulips and place them in the Oasis ring, following all around the sides of the ring, then on top. Here I've grouped the tulips by cultivar and color. Insert pieces of the prunings anywhere you spy a bare spot.

5. It is imperative that you water this wreath arrangement well every day to maximize the longevity of the flowers. The platter will catch any runoff, so don't be stingy.

## ELLEN'S EXTRAS

TULIPS CONTINUE TO GROW EVEN AFTER THEY ARE CUT; THEY ALSO TURN TOWARD THE LIGHT, SO THIS CENTERPIECE WILL CONSTANTLY BE TRANSFORMING ITSELF. IF YOU WANT MORE CONTROL, LEAVE THE STEMS SHORT. THE LONGER YOU KEEP THE STEMS, THE MORE OPPORTUNITY THEY HAVE TO TWIST AND BEND. EXPECT A SLIGHTLY WILD LOOK, AND YOU WON'T BE DISAP-POINTED.

# Permanent Wreath for Fleeting Flowers

Like a favorite vase used year after year, once you have assembled this wreath, it becomes part of your floral design collection. Replace the flowers with the changing seasons and with changing moods, but keep the wreath intact.

## What You Need

Green sheet moss or 5 moss clumps

5 small bunches of fresh flowers (Here I used violets, lilies-of-the-valley, tulips, and lilacs.)

16- to 18-inch-diameter sturdy vine wreath base

Floral spool wire

5 small baskets, with or without handles

5 doilies, tea-size napkins, or linen hand-kerchiefs (These should all be the same color but needn't match.)

5 baby-food or small jelly jars

Fresh-flower food

Water

Clippers

Wire cutters

Hot glue gun and glue sticks

## What You Do

1. Buy or make the heavy vine wreath base. (See "Woven Vine" or "Wrapped Vine" on page 234 for instructions.) Wire each basket to the wreath with pieces of spool wire. These baskets will ultimately hold water jars, so run wire through each basket in several places and try to keep them in a relatively upright position.

2. Glue chunks of moss to the vine around the wreath to brighten it up, then nestle one doily in the bottom of each basket, with the prettiest edge draping over the side. Place a small jar in each basket.

3. Add the flower food to water, following the manufacturer's directions. Carefully add the water to each jar. Then add the flowers and enjoy.

4. When the flowers are ready for the compost heap, wash the jars and doilies and store them with the wreath.

### ELLEN'S EXTRAS

ALWAYS KEEP FRESH FLOWERS OUT OF DIRECT SUNLIGHT TO PROLONG THEIR LIFE. HANG THIS WREATH BESIDE A DOOR RATHER THAN ON IT TO PREVENT WATER SPILLS WITH EVERY ENTRANCE AND EXIT—UNLESS IT IS A DOOR THAT IS RARELY USED. AN INTERIOR WALL IS THE PERFECT ALTERNATIVE.

# Floral Ice Ring

This ice ring will chill the fruit and keep the party warm. I used both garden and wild flowers for lively color. I prefer to use edible flowers, so the adventurous can nibble as the ice melts.

## What You Need

Several handfuls of fresh, edible flowers like violets, pansies, rose petals, calendula, nasturtium, and chive

Fresh leaves (Here I used mint.)

Gelatin mold or Bundt pan

Water

Platter (deep enough to hold water from melting ice)

Dish towel

Clippers

## What You Do

1. Wash and pick over all the flowers and leaves carefully to remove the dirt and insects.

2. Put a layer of flowers and leaves, about an inch high, in the bottom of the mold. Put the flowers face down, but don't bother arranging them too carefully, because they will float around when you add the water.

3. Add 1½ inches of water to the mold and place in the freezer for an hour or two to solidify.

4. Now add another layer of flowers and leaves. Add more water just to cover and refreeze.

5. Continue adding more flowers, leaves, and water, freezing after each addition until the ring is at the height you want. Freeze solid.

6. When the time comes to unmold your floral ice ring, fill the bottom of a sink with hot water and dip the bottom of the mold into the water for five seconds. Shake to see that the ice ring has released. Immediately invert the mold onto the platter you will be using. If the mold is still reluctant to release, dip the dish towel in hot water, ring it out, and drape it over the inverted mold. Give a shake to the platter to help release. Surround the ring with fresh flowers, fruit, and mint leaves. Serve at once or refrigerate briefly until ready to serve.

### ELLEN'S EXTRAS

HERE ARE SOME OTHER WAYS TO DISPLAY YOUR ICE RING. TRY IT IN A PUNCH BOWL INSTEAD OF THAT OLD STANDBY, THE FRUIT RING. OR PLACE THE RING ON A CAKE RACK WITH A TRAY UNDERNEATH. HIDE THE RACK WITH LOTS OF MINT OR OTHER EDIBLE LEAVES BEFORE PLACING THE FOOD AROUND IT. MELTING WATER WILL DRIP DOWN TO THE TRAY BELOW AND NOT ONTO THE FOOD.

# Birch Wreaths in a Centerpiece

*T*hree birch wreaths add drama to the simplest fresh floral arrangement. My shrub rose got pruned to provide the flowers used here. After I toss the roses on the compost pile, I'll stash the wreaths for later use.

## What You Need

3 fresh birch branches, each about 2 to 4 feet tall (available from florists)
5 fresh branches of shrub roses or other flowers you have in abundance
Bucket of water
1 block of green floral foam
Low container into which the floral foam just fits
Floral spool wire
2 candle prongs
2 candles
Clippers
Wire cutters

## What You Do

1. Condition the flowers by recutting the stems and standing them in a bucket of water for eight hours or overnight.

2. Soak the floral foam in water and place it in the container.

3. To make each wreath, hold one birch branch in one hand and grab the tip of the branch with your other hand. Pull the tip down to meet the base, forming an oval. Some of the thinner side

branchlets will escape; let them hang free. Tie the tip to the main stem with spool wire and cut the wire.

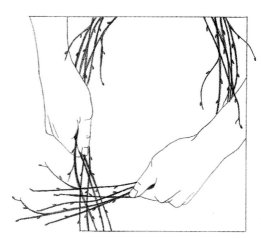

4. Trim the bottom of the branch to a thin point with the clippers. Repeat Step 3 to make two more wreaths.

5. Insert the wreaths into the foam at different angles. Insert the candle prongs into the foam, then place the candles on the prongs.

6. Cut the flower stems as needed and insert them all around the foam, hiding it and the plastic candle prongs.

# A Two-Story Splash

When you need a grand arrangement, put two fresh-flower wreaths together in columnar form. The base, available from a floral supply store or florist, makes construction easy.

## What You Need

Assortment of fresh garden, wild, and
   florist flowers (Here I used 3 stems of
   small wild asters, 24 stems of Queen-
   Anne's-lace, 10 stems of bee balm,
   20 stems of 'Silver King' artemisia,
   20 stems of pastel yarrow, 3 stems of
   baby's-breath, 15 stems of obedient
   plant, 6 stems of mallow, and 12 stems
   of lisianthus.)
38 fresh bamboo stems (or other stems or
   branches), thinner than a pencil and cut
   to the height of your floral stand
Tubular floral stand (available from florists)
2 sturdy rubber bands
2 lengths of ribbon, each 2 to 3 inches
   wide and 1 yard long
2 Oasis foam rings, each 12 inches in
   diameter
Floral preservative
Clippers
Plastic glue (recommended)

## What You Do

1. Stand the floral tube in its base. This one is 24 inches tall, 5 inches in diameter, and made of clear plastic. There are many tubular floral stands on the market, each designed a bit differently. This one pops together, and has one tube in the middle, two adapters, and two plastic trays for the wreaths.

2. Slide two rubber bands down the tube, one 9 inches from the bottom, and one 4 inches from the top. Slip the bamboo under the bands all the way around the column until it is covered, as shown in the illustration on the right.

3. Soak the Oasis foam rings in water to which floral preservative has been added. Remove, drain well, and wipe the bottoms well.

4. Slip the bottom adapter and tray over the tube and down to the base. Glue the bottom of one Oasis ring to the tray. The bottom must be perfectly dry to do this. Arrange the flowers in the bottom tray.

5. Slip the top adapter and tray over the tube. Glue the second Oasis ring to the tray. Arrange the flowers in the top tray. Wrap ribbon over the rubber bands to hide them and tie bows.

### ELLEN'S EXTRAS

IF YOU DON'T HAVE BAMBOO, TRY COVERING THE FLORAL STAND WITH TALL, GREEN LEAVES, LIKE CANNA OR BIRD OF PARADISE. WHEN MAKING THIS PROJECT, CUT THE FLOWER STEMS SHORT, ABOUT 3 TO 6 INCHES. CHOOSE A SIMPLE COLOR SCHEME—HERE I USED VARIATIONS OF PINK, WHITE, AND GREEN.

# Out of Thin Air

Needing no soil, no water, and seemingly, no care, tillandsia plants fascinate us because they defy the rules of the plant world. Their nourishment isn't derived from their roots, but from moisture in the air.

## What You Need

Assorted sizes of tillandsia (Here I used 4 large and 13 small ones.)
2 large handfuls of fresh Spanish moss
16-inch-diameter sturdy vine wreath base
1 piece of thin floral spool wire or floral wire, 12 inches long, for each plant
Brown floral tape
Clippers
Wire cutters

## What You Do

1. Buy or make the vine wreath base. (See "Woven Vine" or "Wrapped Vine" on page 234 for instructions.) Here I've used wisteria vine, but any thick vine will do. This wreath can be wild and irregular, which is certainly easier to make than a perfectly even one.

2. Wrap each piece of wire with floral tape. This will help disguise the wire when it's on the wreath. To use floral tape, stretch it out gently and overlap it as you go. The tape will stick to itself but not directly to the wire.

### WREATHMAKER'S ❧ WISDOM ❦

Tillandsia plants can last for years if treated properly. Because they get their moisture from the air, tillandsia wreaths should hang in a very bright, humid spot. A sunny bathroom is perfect. If your spot isn't humid, mist the plants daily with a plant mister. Do not soak them. After a plant blooms, it usually sends out small offshoots and the mother plant dies. You may have to re-distribute the plants after several years, removing any dead ones.

To use fewer plants in this project, add more moss and pieces of wild-looking bark, such as cork bark. Purchase bark where you buy the plants. Simply glue pieces to the wreath.

3. For each tillandsia, wrap a piece of covered wire between the leaves around its base, as shown in the illustration on the opposite page. Leave a tail on each end of the wire to be used for attaching the plant to the wreath.

4. Now suspend the tillandsia from the vine wreath on their wires, twisting the wires to secure. Start with the biggest plants first and arrange them toward the bottom of the wreath. Attach them so they face outward toward the viewer, or upward. Then wire on the smaller air plants around the wreath, letting several hang down. Cut off the extraneous wire.

5. Fill in the bare spots with fresh Spanish moss. Allow some moss to drip down from the wreath to give it a wild look and to hide the suspension wires.

# Fresh Winter Wreath

*F*or a lift during the dreary days of winter, use long-lasting fresh flowers to decorate a simple wreath of evergreens. The heart shapes of the red and pink anthuriums are perfect for a Valentine celebration. Add a bow for a different look.

## What You Need

30 cuttings of evergreens, each 8 to
  10 inches long (Here I used blue spruce.)
4 fresh red anthuriums
4 fresh pink anthuriums
3 stems of fresh white broom
10-inch-diameter wire wreath frame with
  clamps
Small Oasis Igloo
12-inch piece of floral spool wire
Clippers
Wire cutters
Pliers (optional)

## What You Do

1. Divide the evergreens into ten piles of three cuttings each. Take the first pile, position it in a clamp on the wreath frame and clamp the stems tightly. If desired, use pliers to bend the clamps. (See "Wire Wreath Frame with Clamps" on page 236.)

2. Take the next pile, lay it over the stems of the first pile, and clamp it in place. Continue until all ten piles are used.

3. Soak the Oasis Igloo in water for 15 minutes. Remove and let drain. The Igloo has holes around the outside base. Thread the wire through the holes and tie the Igloo securely to the wreath. Position the Igloo so that it is on one side of the wreath rather than on the bottom.

4. Before adding the flowers, hang the wreath; this will make it easier to see how the design will actually appear. If the temperature in your region drops below 38°F, hang the wreath indoors to work on it.

5. Insert the anthuriums in the Igloo, adding first one color, then the other. Shorten the stems as necessary. The shortest stem here was 3 inches long, used in the center to help hide the Oasis Igloo. The longest was 10 inches long. Cut the stems of broom into shorter lengths and use to fill in around the anthuriums.

6. You must add water to the Igloo every day. To do this it's best to take the wreath over to the sink, pour water into the Igloo, and let it drain. The life of this decoration is about two weeks indoors. The evergreens will still be good after the flowers have died and can be reused with another decoration.

# Poinsettia Wreath and Ivy Wreath Topiary

This wreath does double duty—hanging on a wall or becoming the centerpiece for a holiday table. Add to the holiday feel with a topiary wreath. This one is made from a trailing, small-leaf ivy.

## What You Need for the Wreath

1 or 2 pots of fresh poinsettias with a total of 12 to 14 blooms (Here I used plants of two different colors.)
15 fresh mini carnations
15 cuttings of fresh holly leaves (berries aren't necessary) or other greens
4 stems of fresh waxflowers
1 candle
1 candleholder
Matches
Bucket of water
15-inch-diameter Oasis foam ring
Clippers

## What You Do

1. Put the candle in the holder and light the candle. Cut a poinsettia bract from the plant, leaving a 4-inch stem. A white, milky sap will exude from the cut. Singe the cut end of the bract over the candle flame for about five seconds.

2. Place the poinsettia bract in a bucket of water to condition for about four hours. Continue to seal and condition all of the bracts in this manner.

3. Place the other flowers and greens in water to condition them.

4. Fill a clean sink with water. Soak the Oasis foam ring in water for 30 minutes. Remove the ring and hold it upright over the sink to drain. It may continue to drip for some time. Wipe the bottom of the ring and place it on your work surface.

5. This is a lush arrangement but easy to do. Place the largest poinsettias first. Here the coral bracts were bigger and fewer than the light pink. I inserted them first in the ring. Then place the smaller, pink bracts around the ring, spacing them evenly.

### ELLEN'S EXTRAS

THE INDOOR POINSETTIA WREATH WILL LAST AT LEAST 2 WEEKS, BUT YOU MUST ADD WATER REGULARLY. EVERY OTHER DAY, TAKE DOWN THE WREATH AND PLACE ON THE SINK DRAINBOARD. POUR ABOUT A CUP OF WATER INTO THE OASIS FOAM AROUND THE WREATH, AS IF YOU WERE WATERING A PLANT. LET THE WATER SOAK IN FOR 30 MINUTES, CHECK FOR DRIPS, AND REHANG.

6. Cut the carnation stems short, to 3 to 4 inches, and insert them around the ring. Now fill in with the holly or other greens, covering any bare spots that you see.

7. Cut the waxflower stems to about 6 inches. You will get several good pieces out of each stem. Insert them around the wreath. Before hanging, hold the wreath over the sink again to catch any drips.

## What You Need for the Topiary

1 large, trailing, potted, small-leaf ivy plant (several strands should be at least 18 inches long)
1 handful of tiny cones, like larch or hemlock
44 inches of 18-gauge wire
2 yards of wire-edged ribbon (optional)
Gold spray paint
About 3 feet of very thin gold wire or thread
Clippers
Wire cutters

## What You Do

1. To make the topiary frame, form a 10-inch-diameter circle with the 18-gauge wire, leaving 6-inch tails at each end. Twist the wires together and then bend to make two legs.

### ELLEN'S EXTRAS

THIS TOPIARY WILL CONTINUE TO GROW IF CARED FOR AND WATERED. IVY LIKES A COOL SITUATION WITH MOIST (NOT WET) SOIL. REMOVE THE DECORATIONS AFTER CHRISTMAS. PRUNE ANY STRANDS THAT GET UNRULY AND ROOT THEM IN WATER TO START NEW PLANTS.

2. Water the ivy and insert the frame in the center of the pot by pushing the legs into the soil. Take the longest strand of ivy and wrap it carefully around the frame, going up from the bottom to the top and along one side, as far as it will go. Wrap another long strand around the other side of the frame, going from bottom to top. Continue wrapping strands on each side, leaving some of the shortest strands to cover the soil in front of the pot.

3. If you choose to decorate, make a bow with the ribbon, leaving long tails. (See "Making a Bow" on page 243 for instructions.) Wire the bow to the top of the wreath and wind the tails around the wreath, draping them down.

4. Spray the cones gold. When they are dry, wrap the gold wire around the cones, between the bottom "petals," and make tiny hooks for hanging. Or tie the thread into a loop around the bottom petals and hang the cones on the wreath.

# A Living Wreath

There are many ways to make this wreath, and they all require patience. Here, small divisions of sedum are planted in a moss-filled ring. The sedum must grow roots before the wreath can be hung.

## What You Need

15 to 20 pieces of fresh sedum, different varieties or all one kind (Here I used enough to make a 16-inch-diameter finished wreath.)
10 to 12 handfuls of fresh sphagnum moss
10 × 54-inch piece of chicken wire
Stick or chopstick
Clippers
Wire cutters

## What You Do

1. Whether you dig sedum from your garden or buy it, divide the clumps into stems. Let cuttings without roots sit out for two days to allow the cut end to form a callus.

2. Wet the moss and wring it out. Lay it in a strip down the middle of the wire.

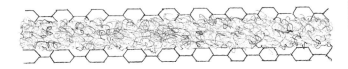

3. Fold over the top and bottom of the wire to envelope the moss. Bend the wire to form a tube. Interlace the cut ends of the wire to hold them together.

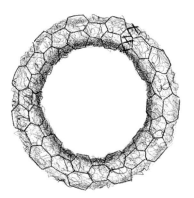

4. Poke holes in the moss with the stick and plant each piece of sedum in a hole. Keep the wreath in the sun and water well. It should show signs of new growth in a couple of weeks.

5. If you are hanging the sedum wreath, you must take it down every few days, or when dry, and water well. Let it drain before rehanging.

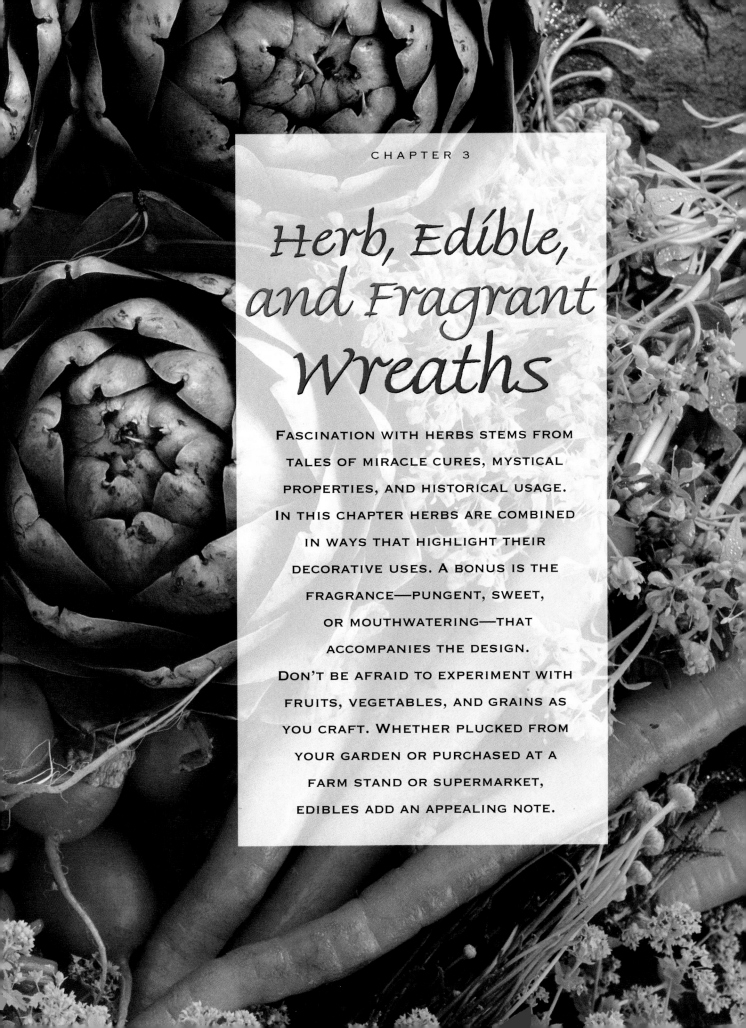

CHAPTER 3

# Herb, Edible, and Fragrant Wreaths

FASCINATION WITH HERBS STEMS FROM
TALES OF MIRACLE CURES, MYSTICAL
PROPERTIES, AND HISTORICAL USAGE.
IN THIS CHAPTER HERBS ARE COMBINED
IN WAYS THAT HIGHLIGHT THEIR
DECORATIVE USES. A BONUS IS THE
FRAGRANCE—PUNGENT, SWEET,
OR MOUTHWATERING—THAT
ACCOMPANIES THE DESIGN.
DON'T BE AFRAID TO EXPERIMENT WITH
FRUITS, VEGETABLES, AND GRAINS AS
YOU CRAFT. WHETHER PLUCKED FROM
YOUR GARDEN OR PURCHASED AT A
FARM STAND OR SUPERMARKET,
EDIBLES ADD AN APPEALING NOTE.

# Thyme After Time

*H*ave fun punning the title of this wreath: "Don't Waste My Thyme" or "Thyme on My Hands." The "As Thyme Goes By" sign is crucial, since most people won't recognize the dried thyme unless it is identified.

## What You Need

60 to 80 stems of dried thyme, any variety or mixed

Small clusters of pepperberries and hydrangea (optional)

14-inch-diameter sturdy vine wreath base

Flat white spray paint

Parts from old watches and clocks

Small sign, hand-lettered or computer-generated

Clippers

Hot glue gun and glue sticks

Thick craft glue or epoxy

Small screwdriver

## What You Do

1. Buy or make the vine wreath base. (See "Woven Vine" or "Wrapped Vine" on page 234 for instructions.) Spray it white and let it dry.

2. Collect inexpensive watches or clocks. Search flea markets and garage sales for nonworking discards. For the most interesting inner workings, select the wind-up variety.

3. Take the timepieces apart with the screwdriver. Each individual spring and gear can become a decoration. Keep tiny parts attached to bigger pieces where possible so they don't get hidden.

4. Hot-glue the dried thyme in clusters around the wreath, then glue on the watch and clock pieces with craft glue or epoxy. (Hot glue doesn't hold metal pieces.)

5. Add bits of color, if desired, with pepperberries and hydrangea by hot-gluing them to the vine. Tuck in your sign and glue it in place.

### ELLEN'S EXTRAS

IF YOU GROW OR HAVE A SOURCE FOR FRESH THYME, YOU DON'T HAVE TO WAIT FOR IT TO DRY BEFORE USING IT IN THIS WREATH. GLUE THE THYME TO THE VINE WREATH BASE WHILE STILL FRESH AND LET IT DRY IN PLACE BEFORE ADDING THE TIMEPIECES. YOU WILL GET LESS CRUMBLING THAT WAY. REMEMBER THAT ANY PLANT SHRINKS WHEN DRIED, SO PUT ON ABOUT TWICE AS MUCH FRESH THYME AS YOU THINK YOU NEED, OTHERWISE, IT WILL LOOK SPARSE WHEN DRIED. LET THE WREATH LIE FLAT ON A TABLE WHILE THE THYME IS DRYING TO ACHIEVE THE NEATEST RESULTS. IT WILL TAKE AT LEAST A WEEK FOR THE THYME TO DRY. DRYING TIME VARIES BASED ON WHERE YOU PUT THE WREATH, HOW HUMID YOUR HOUSE IS, AND HOW FRESH THE THYME IS.

# Cinnamon Stick Basket and Lavender Edibles

*I* set out to make a hexagonal cinnamon stick wreath, but I made a detour. When the frame was finished, it cried out to be a basket, so I added a stick across the middle and kept going. The lavender wreath turned out as I had planned.

## What You Need for the Stick Basket

19 cinnamon sticks, each 15 to 16 inches long
9 dried orange slices
4 dried lemon slices
5 whole nutmegs
1 ribbon bow (optional)
Clippers
Hot glue gun and glue sticks
Tape measure or ruler

## What You Do

1. Cut or break 18 of the long sticks to 10 inches. Do not break the remaining stick. Reserve all the cut pieces.

2. Place three 10-inch cinnamon sticks as shown below. Then lay three other 10-inch sticks across them. Adjust the shape until it is even. Glue each stick in place at the joints.

3. Build up two more layers of 10-inch cinnamon sticks on top of the first layer and glue them together. Now glue the long, unbroken stick across the middle to designate the basket rim.

4. Glue some of the reserved 5- to 6-inch sticks across the basket in pleasing patterns. Continue to cut or break the sticks horizontally or vertically to the sizes you need.

5. Glue on the oranges, lemons, and nutmegs where desired. Here I've glued most of the materials to the surface, but some slices are glued to the sticks in the middle layer.

6. Glue on a bow, if desired. Here the bow hides a mistake I made when I broke my last cinnamon stick—I had to piece it together. Shhhhh!

## What You Need for the Lavender Edibles

70 stems of dried lavender
10- or 11-inch-diameter purchased willow wreath base

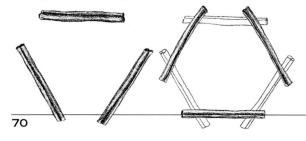

7 dried orange slices
5 stems of pink pepperberries
Floral tape
Clippers
Hot glue gun and glue sticks

## What You Do

1. Divide the lavender into seven bundles of ten stems each. Hold each bundle together by wrapping it with floral tape 5 inches from the tips. Then cut the bundles to 9 inches long, reserving the stem ends.

2. Glue on the lavender bundles diagonally across the wreath base. As you glue on each bundle, its stems will hide the previous bundle's tape.

3. Glue the oranges to the wreath between the lavender bundles. Ring the inside of the wreath with pepperberries, gluing them to the lavender stems.

4. Tuck the reserved, bare lavender stems into the wreath near each orange. The finished wreath will measure about 15 inches.

# Four Times the Herbs

*E*ach small circle features a different herb: love-in-a-mist for flavoring, bee balm for tea, lady's-mantle for bathing, and pennyroyal for insect repellency.

## What You Need

Assortment of herbs: 4 varieties for the small wreaths and several others to decorate the center
4 vine wreath bases, each 8 inches in diameter
Floral spool wire
Clippers
Wire cutters
Hot glue gun and glue sticks

## What You Do

1. Buy or make four vine wreath bases. (See "Woven Vine" or "Wrapped Vine" on page 234 for instructions.)

2. Bind pairs of wreath bases together with the spool wire, as shown below. Then bind the four bases together in the center with more spool wire. Tie the spool wire onto one of the bases.

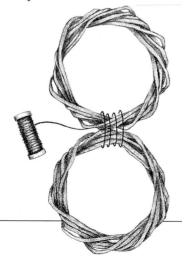

### ELLEN'S EXTRAS

A THREE- OR FOUR-PART WREATH IS AN EXCELLENT WAY TO HIGHLIGHT HERBS OF ONE BOTANICAL SPECIES. TRY FOUR DIFFERENT MINTS OR FOUR ALLIUMS. OR USE FOUR DIFFERENT TEA HERBS, FOUR MEDICINAL HERBS, OR FOUR CULINARY HERBS. THE CHOICES ARE LIMITED ONLY BY YOUR IMAGINATION.

3. Cut the stems of the herbs to 4 inches. Take three to four stems of one variety and attach them to one of the wreath bases by wrapping the cluster with the spool wire. (See "Single-Wire Frame" on page 235 for instructions.) Continue adding the same kind of herb and wrapping it in place until you have gone completely around one wreath.

4. Wrap the other three wreath bases in the same way, each with a different herb. The last base is hardest to wrap where the bases meet; but don't worry, the center decoration will hide any problem areas. Cut the decorative herbs very short and glue them to the center of the wreath.

# corn-and-wheat wheel

*It* looks good enough to eat, and it *will* be eaten if you leave this wreath on an unprotected door. This wheel also makes a dramatic centerpiece on a large dining table, flanked by red tapers in brass holders.

## What You Need

1 dried sunflower seed head (Here it is 7 inches in diameter.)

38 ears of decorative dried strawberry corn

19 dried red globe amaranth heads

38 stems of black-bearded wheat

19 small clusters of red pepperberries

Circle of corrugated cardboard, cut from a carton (Here it is 14 inches in diameter.)

Floral pin

Spray paint in moss green (optional)

Spray shellac, varnish, or polyurethane (optional)

Clippers

Hot glue gun and glue sticks

Utility knife

## What You Do

1. Determine the diameter of your wreath by measuring the diameter of the sunflower head and adding the length of four ears of corn. Use the utility knife to cut the cardboard circle to size. Size the circle so the cardboard won't show after the wreath is made. (The finished wreath, shown in the photo on the opposite page, is 26 inches in diameter.)

2. Make a wreath hanger with the floral pin and attach it to the back of the cardboard circle. (See "How to Hang a Wreath" on page 240.) Then spray the front of the cardboard with the paint, if desired. This will hide any little spots of cardboard that might show through the completed wreath.

3. Glue the sunflower head to the middle of the cardboard circle. All of the materials in this project are glued onto the cardboard. Use lots of glue and apply pressure until the glue dries. You want to ensure a strong bond because some of these materials are heavy.

4. With the leaves pointing outward, glue 19 ears of corn in a ring around the sunflower. Trim off some of the leaves if they seem to overpower the corn.

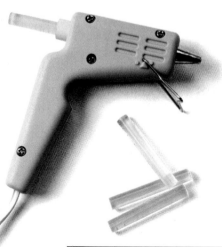

5. Take all the leaves off the remaining 19 ears of corn. Glue the bottom of each ear to the bottom of an ear that's already in place. Glue the corn directly to the cardboard to hold it securely; make sure you are not simply gluing it to a flimsy leaf.

6. Glue a globe amaranth head between each of the first 19 ears of corn.

7. Cut off the stems of the wheat. Glue two wheat heads facing outward between each ear of corn in the outer circle. Then glue a small cluster of pepperberries on top of each pair of wheat heads.

8. Spray the wreath with a protective coating of shellac, varnish, or polyurethane, if desired.

# A New Twist

$\mathcal{M}$y husband's bread is coveted by our family and throughout the county. I scarfed some of his dough to make this bread wreath. The result is that no one will taste the ambrosial flavor of what would have been "Dr. Ben's Homemade Challah."

## What You Need

Dried wheat and a few stems of bread-seasoning herbs, like dill and poppy

Bread dough from your favorite recipe or frozen bread dough from the supermarket

About ½ cup of flour

Baking sheet

Canola or corn oil cooking spray

1 egg yolk mixed with 1 tablespoon of water

Pastry brush

Cooling rack

Polyurethane spray, low gloss or glossy, as you prefer

Rubber band

2 yards of paper ribbon

Floral spool wire

Clippers

Scissors

Wire cutters

## What You Do

1. Allow the dough to rise once, then punch it down.

2. Sprinkle flour on a clean work surface. Divide the dough in half and roll each half into a long, thin rope. The ropes should be 1 to 2 inches thick.

3. Join the ropes at the top by pressing the top ends together. Gently twist the ropes together, one over the other. Press the ends together.

4. Lightly grease the baking sheet with the cooking spray and form the twisted rope dough into a circle on the sheet. Press the bottom ends together.

5. Allow the dough to rise again on the baking sheet. Using the pastry brush, paint the surface of the dough with the egg mixture. This will make it shiny after baking.

6. Bake the bread according to your recipe (or the package directions if you are using frozen dough) but watch carefully. This wreath will bake much faster than a normal loaf of bread. Remove the bread from the oven when golden brown and let cool.

7. The bread will be too fresh to hang for at least a week. You must let it get stale to allow time for the inside to dry out and to give it strength. Place the bread on a cooling rack on the top of your refrigerator or any other warm spot. If it's very humid in your house, be sure to watch for signs of mold as the bread is drying. If necessary, let the bread dry in a very slow oven set at 150°F for two hours.

8. When the bread is dry, spray all the surfaces with polyurethane. This coating will protect it against bugs and mold.

9. Make a small bouquet of dried wheat and bread-seasoning herbs and secure it with the rubber band. Trim the bottoms of the stems.

10. Make a bow using the ribbon and 2 feet of spool wire. (See "Making a Bow" on page 243 for instructions.) Wrap the bow around the herb bouquet and use the same wire to secure it to the wreath.

# Oats, Beans, and Barley Grow

*T*he path to my home leads straight to the kitchen. In true farmhouse fashion, the front door is never used. A wreath of dried edibles adds to the atmosphere when "nothin's cookin'."

## What You Need

180 stems of dried oats, barley, wheat, and sea oats (any combination)

8 freeze-dried red potatoes or dried red peppers

4 dried okra pods

About 30 dried beans in the pods (Here I used purple hyacinth beans.)

50-inch length of 16- or 18-gauge wire

Floral tape

Floral spool wire

Clippers

Wire cutters

Hot glue gun and glue sticks

## What You Do

1. Make an 11-inch square with the 16-gauge wire. (The finished size of the wreath will be 15 inches square.) Wrap the leftover wire around the first side you formed to hold the square in place. Wrap the square with the floral tape to cover the wire.

2. Make bundles of 15 stems of grains. Lay one bundle on top of the wire, with grain tips extending

## WREATHMAKER'S WISDOM

*Look for beans with red or mottled pods or with red seeds. Pick or buy them when they are plump and mature. Slit the pods open on the side opposite from where the beans are attached. You'll find out which side this is after you make your first mistake. The beans can air-dry in place on the wreath, or dry on high in your microwave on microwavable paper for approximately 30 seconds. Experiment with the length of time for your beans. It may be necessary to put a dab of glue on each bean to attach it firmly to the open pod after the beans and pods have dried.*

*The glorious vine climbing around the wooden door in the photograph on the opposite page is the annual hyacinth bean vine; it is used in some Asian cuisines. Purple hyacinth beans are available from Shepherd's Garden Seeds. (See "Seed Sources" on page 246 for information.)*

slightly over the corner. Secure the bundle to the frame with spool wire.

3. Take the next bunch of grains, lay it over the stems of the first bunch, and continue wrapping with the spool wire.

4. Continue around the frame in this manner, cutting the stems as necessary so they don't stick out of the ends of the wreath. Each side will use about three bundles.

5. Place your decorative goodies around the wreath in a pleasing pattern and glue them in place. Glue the heavier items like the potatoes and okra toward the base of the wreath. (Don't expect a potato to hang happily from one stalk of oats or barley.) Then glue on the dried bean pods.

# Fruited Eucalyptus

The aroma of preserved eucalyptus freshens the air with its pungency. Here this tried-and-true material is combined with freeze-dried fruits and vegetables for something new.

## What You Need

18 to 25 stems of preserved green
    eucalyptus
8 to 10 dried apple and dried orange slices
6 to 8 dried pomegranate slices
1 freeze-dried papaya half
10 freeze-dried strawberries (optional)
10 stems of roundleaf oregano (optional)
12-inch-diameter wire wreath base
Floral spool wire
Clippers
Wire cutters
Hot glue gun and glue sticks

## What You Do

1. Buy or make the wire wreath base. (See "Single-Wire Frame" on page 235. Also see "How to Dry Fruit" on page 241 for instructions on how to dry the apples, oranges, and pomegranates; or buy them already dried.)

2. To make the eucalyptus wreath, cut the eucalyptus stems to about 8 inches, measuring from the tips. When you get to the bottom of the stems, discard any unsightly bits. Each stem will give you eight or more cuttings.

3. Tie one end of the spool wire to the frame. Make a bundle of seven eucalyptus cuttings, placing the nicest-looking cuttings on top. Place the bundle on the frame and wrap the wire around it tightly. (See "Single-Wire Frame" on page 235 for instructions.)

4. Place another bundle of eucalyptus cuttings on the frame and wrap tightly. This bundle will hide the stems of the previous bundle. Of course, the more bundles you use and the more stems in each bundle, the larger and fuller the wreath will be. Continue tying on bundles until the wreath is complete, then tie off and cut the spool wire.

5. Glue the papaya or other large fruit on first, attaching it near the frame. Then glue the other fruit around the wreath in a pleasing arrangement. End with sprigs of roundleaf oregano, if desired.

## ELLEN'S EXTRAS

FEEL FREE TO IMPROVISE WHEN MAKING THIS OR ANY WREATH YOU SEE IN THIS BOOK. FOR EXAMPLE, HERE YOU CAN USE SEVERAL WHOLE DRIED POMEGRANATES OR A BRIGHT BOW INSTEAD OF THE PAPAYA. INSTEAD OF ROUNDLEAF OREGANO, TRY SPRIGS OF DRIED HYDRANGEA. INSTEAD OF THE STRAWBERRIES, USE RED PEPPERBERRIES.

# Pasta Makers' Dream

*One ring of oregano, one of basil; a decoration of garlic, pepper, and tomato with a fettuccine bow—be careful no one tries to throw it in the pot for an instant dinner!*

## What You Need

50 stems of dried oregano
50 stems of dried basil, preferably the dark opal variety
3 heads of garlic
Small dried or fresh peppers, like cayenne
2 or 3 stems of fresh cherry tomatoes (optional)
14- to 16-inch-diameter vine wreath base, round or oval
10- to 12-inch-diameter vine wreath base, round or oval
Floral spool wire
1 handful of uncooked fettuccine
10 strands of natural raffia
Polyurethane spray
Clippers
Wire cutters
Hot glue gun and glue sticks

## What You Do

1. Buy or make the vine wreath bases. (See "Woven Vine" or "Wrapped Vine" on page 234 for instructions.)

2. Wrap the oregano to the larger wreath base with the spool wire a few stems at a time, making sure the leaves cover the stems of the previous bundle. Continue adding oregano until the entire wreath base is covered. Do the same with the basil on the smaller wreath base. Then attach the two wreaths to each other at their tops with spool wire.

3. Gather the handful of fettuccine into a bundle and tie it in the center with three strands of raffia. Make a simple bow with the raffia. Spray the fettuccine with polyurethane to protect it from bugs. Let it dry, then turn the bundle over and spray the other side.

4. With the remaining seven strands of raffia, tie the fettuccine to the top center of the double wreath and make a simple bow. Fettucine is fragile, so take care.

5. Glue the garlic around the basil wreath in individual cloves. Glue the peppers across the top of the wreath near the bow. If the peppers are small, like cayenne, you can use fresh ones—they will dry right on the wreath.

6. Since I designed this wreath in late summer and had loads of cherry tomatoes in the garden, I draped a few pieces of tomato vine around the wreath for added appeal. The tomatoes will get plucked off very soon and nibbled by passersby; I know I'll be the first in line.

# Sages and Mints

*E*ach wreath highlights herbs in one botanical family. Both are made in the same way. Vary the proportions based on which herbs you have on hand.

## What You Need for 1 Wreath

Assortment of dried sages or mints (For the sage wreath I used blue, gray, and clary sage for the base and scarlet sage for decoration. For the mint wreath I used mountain mint and spearmint for the base and lion's-ear and lemon mint for decoration.)

14-gauge wire

Floral spool wire

Clippers

Wire cutters

Hot glue gun and glue sticks

## What You Do

1. Make an 8- to 10-inch diameter circle with the 14-gauge wire and twist the wire ends together to fasten. (See "Single-Wire Frame" on page 235 for instructions.) Wrap on the base herbs in clusters of three to five stems, with the clusters all going in the same direction around the wire circle.

2. Glue the decorative herbs around the wreath in a pleasing pattern.

# All in the Allium Family

Onions, garlic, chives, and decorative giant allium are all in the same family. Gather as many examples as you can from your garden or from local markets to complete this wreath.

## What You Need

Any mix of 80 to 90 assorted small onions, shallots, top onions, and garlic heads (whatever you can find)
Dried chive flowers
Dried seed heads of garlic chives
3 dried seed heads of decorative giant allium
18-inch square of green sheet moss
14-inch-diameter extruded foam wreath base
8 floral pins
1 floral pick for each onion you are using (3-inch-long picks for small onions and 5-inch-long picks for larger onions)
Clippers
Hot glue gun and glue sticks
Paring knife

## What You Do

1. If the wreath base has sharply angled sides, round them off at the top and bottom with the paring knife.

2. Cover the wreath base with the sheet moss, bringing the moss down over the sides and trimming as necessary. Pin the moss in place with the floral pins.

3. Remove the wires from the floral picks. Stick a pick in the bottom of an onion and push the other end into the wreath base. Go all around the wreath with one kind of onion, using about 14 onions, then switch to another kind. Use what you have the most of first.

4. Put the varieties you have the least of on the surface of the wreath where they will show. When the surface is covered, add materials on longer picks to give a three-dimensional look. Glue chive flowers and seed heads of garlic chives into the empty spaces.

5. Cut the stems of the giant allium seed heads to a point and insert them into the wreath base—two in the center and one toward the bottom, as shown in the photo on the opposite page.

### ELLEN'S EXTRAS

MANY OF THESE ONIONS WILL DRY IN PLACE BECAUSE THEY ARE SMALL. THE COOLER THE HANGING SITE, THE LONGER THE WREATH WILL LAST. AND IF THE ONIONS ARE NOT COMPLETELY TOUCHING EACH OTHER, SO MUCH THE BETTER. BECAUSE THE ONIONS ARE INSERTED ON PICKS, THEY CAN BE REMOVED AND REPLACED. THINK OF THIS AS A SEASONAL WREATH WITH A FOUR- TO SIX-MONTH LIFE SPAN, RATHER THAN ONE THAT WILL LAST "FOREVER."

# Please Don't Eat the Wreath

*W*hen I roam the produce department with the eye of a floral designer rather than the eye of a cook, certain shapes and colors stand out. The supermarket is an excellent source for fresh materials to use in wreaths—especially in winter when my garden is asleep.

## What You Need

Assortment of vegetables and other edibles (Here I used 1 bunch of dried wheat, 1 bunch of long carrots with leafy tops, 15-inch-long cinnamon sticks, dried red peppers, artichokes, small lemons, and mushrooms.)

18-inch-diameter wreath base of fresh greens, like arborvitae

Floral spool wire

1 ready-made bow or 3 yards of colorful ribbon

Floral picks, 5 to 7 inches long

Clippers

Wire cutters

## What You Do

1. Buy or make the wreath base. (See "How to Make Your Own Wreath Base" on page 234 for instructions.)

2. Divide the wheat in half and place the two bundles end to end, overlapping by 6 inches. Wrap tightly with spool wire to start the swag.

3. Cut the tops off the carrots, leaving a 4-inch stem. Divide the carrots with the leafy tops in half. Place each half on top of the wheat, end to end, and wrap the carrots tightly to the wheat with the spool wire to complete the swag.

## WREATHMAKER'S WISDOM

*I started this wreath with arborvitae because it is an evergreen that lasts for months without dropping. (I also happen to have a huge hedge of it!)*

*When using floral picks, if the little wire isn't needed, remove it. Pare the blunt end of the pick to a point with clippers or a paring knife. Now you have two sharp ends, one to go into the fruit or vegetable and one to insert into the wreath.*

*To prolong the life of the edibles, select sound, firm specimens. Wash them in a solution of 1 gallon of water and ½ cup of bleach. Soak the carrots in clear water overnight. Dry all of the edibles, then dip them in acrylic floor wax to coat. Let them dry before using them on the wreath.*

*Mist the wreath frequently to keep the greens fresh. This wreath will last longer in a cool environment where it will not freeze, such as in a protected location outdoors.*

4. Wire the swag to the wreath at an angle at the two o'clock position, using the photo as a guide. Using either a ready-made bow or one you've made from the ribbon (see "Making a Bow" on page 243), tie the bow to the wreath, covering the wrapped wires of the swag.

5. Attach all the other materials to floral picks and insert them deep into the thickness of the greenery on the wreath base. Wrap with extra lengths of spool wire to secure, if necessary.

# A Is for Apple

Small apples, such as 'Lady' apples or crabapples, adorn this colorful fall wreath. I don't recommend this wreath for a door that gets heavy use.

## What You Need

1 or more varieties of round, small apples (with stems, if possible)
Dried apple slices
10 to 12 fresh or dried lemonleaf (salal) leaves
About 8 yards of 18-gauge wire
Black spray paint
1 ready-made bow (optional)
Gold thread
Clippers
Wire cutters
Hot glue gun and glue sticks

## What You Do

1. Make a 16-inch-diameter circle with the 18-gauge wire. Then weave the remaining wire in and out of the circle until you use up all the wire. As you weave, leave loops and irregularities of different sizes, as shown in the photo.

2. Spray three coats of black paint over the wire circle, letting it dry thoroughly between coats.

3. Hang the wire circle in place. If you are using a bow, attach it now, before you begin to add the fruit.

4. Push the smallest apples into place between the loops of the wire. For additional security, tie pieces of gold thread to each stem and then to a nearby wire. Or use some thread to dangle a few apples in the center, like the old bobbing-for-apples game. After placing the apples, if you have exposed some silver wire, spray a puddle of black paint in a disposable dish. Use a cotton swab to dab the paint where needed.

5. Glue on the apple slices and lemonleaf (salal) foliage around the wreath.

# copper-clad Artichokes

*A*rtichokes from the supermarket serve as well as artichokes from the garden, and copper paint is as close as your hardware store. This festive wreath also serves as a centerpiece.

## what You Need

19 fresh artichokes
Green sheet moss, about 10 inches square (doesn't need to be in one piece)
46 dried orange globe amaranths
14-inch-diameter extruded foam wreath base
Copper spray paint
Spool of #28 copper wire
Clippers
Wire cutters
Hot glue gun and glue sticks

## what You Do

1. Allow the artichokes to dry by spreading them out in a warm, dry spot. One good place is on a cookie rack on top of your refrigerator. They will dry in about two weeks.

2. With the clippers, cut the stem of an artichoke to a point. Put glue on the end and insert it into the inside edge of the wreath base. Continue until you have encircled the inner ring of the wreath with seven artichokes.

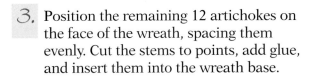

3. Position the remaining 12 artichokes on the face of the wreath, spacing them evenly. Cut the stems to points, add glue, and insert them into the wreath base.

4. Lightly mist all of the artichokes with the copper spray paint. When the paint has dried, glue pieces of green sheet moss around the edges of the wreath and between the artichokes as needed to hide the foam.

5. Cut the stems off the globe amaranths. Glue on pairs of flowers between the artichokes, as shown in the photo.

6. Take the spool of copper wire and weave it all around the wreath like a big web, going under, over, and around.

# CHAPTER 4

# Theme Wreaths

A favorite hobby, a personal
celebration, a botanical pun, a
memory—all spark ideas for a theme
wreath. In this chapter the props
are sometimes as important as the
natural materials.

One of my favorite theme wreaths is
the "Family Tree," shown on page 96,
which hangs over my dressing table.
I made it to enchant my little niece
with stories of her grandmother
and great-grandmother.

Allow my inventions here to suggest
themes; personalize these wreaths
to make them your own.

# Family Tree

Transfer pictures from an album, where they are rarely seen, to your wall for all to enjoy. Give the gift of family to your new daughter-in-law or to your grandchild who lives far away.

## What You Need

- 8 to 11 clumps of dried moss or a 14-inch square of green sheet moss (doesn't need to be in one piece)
- 18- to 20-inch-long tree branch or several thin twigs (Here I used birch.)
- 5 small family photos
- 5 small frames
- 1 floral pin
- 1 corrugated cardboard oval, cut from an old carton (The oval here is 11 × 14 inches.)
- Spool of 28-gauge gold or silver wire to match the frames (available at craft stores)
- Clippers
- Scissors
- Wire cutters
- Hot glue gun and glue sticks
- Double-sided tape (optional)

## What You Do

1. Affix the photos to the frames, trimming if necessary. Some frames come with backs and the mechanics to do this. The frames used here are from a craft shop, are very inexpensive, and have no back. I affixed the photos with double-sided tape.

2. Push in the floral pin ½ inch from the top edge of the cardboard and bend it back to make a hanger. (See "How to Hang a Wreath" on page 240.)

3. Glue moss around the oval, extending it over the edges of the cardboard.

4. Attach the picture frames to the wreath with the wire. To do this, wrap the wire catty-corner around the frames and around the wreath, much like a gift package. Leave extra wire to make a bow or spirals (roll the ends around a pencil and release), if desired.

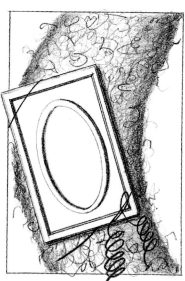

5. Position the twigs on one side of the wreath in a way that won't hide the photos. Tie them to the wreath with additional wire.

# welcoming the Bride

As lovely and delicate as the bride, this wedding wreath decorates the front door of your home, announcing the festivities and greeting all who enter. This wreath is made in a narrow oval, patterned after the glass insert in the door.

## what You Need

50 twigs, each 10 to 16 inches long
2 to 4 stems of fresh asparagus fern, purchased or cut from a plant
2 stems of fresh Baker fern
6 fresh phalaenopsis orchids (purchase in tubes of water from the florist)
16-gauge wire
Brown floral tape
White or ivory ribbon, 1½ to 3 inches wide (Here I've used 3 yards of three different silky ribbons.)
22- or 24-gauge floral spool wire
Clippers
Scissors
Wire cutters

## what You Do

1. Make the wreath base by forming an oval or circle out of the 16-gauge wire. Twist the ends together to hold. Here the dimensions of the wire oval are 12 inches at its widest point and 18 inches at its highest point to make a wreath that will end up 24 inches wide and 32 inches high.

2. Wrap the wire base with the floral tape, completely covering the wire. Then divide the twigs into ten equal bundles.

### WREATHMAKER'S ❧ WISDOM ❧

Prune twigs from any shrub or tree with fine branches. Of course each type of twig gives a different look to the wreath, but I haven't yet met a twig I didn't like. These were cut in the spring just before the leaves broke out. If you are cutting in the summer, you will have to strip off the leaves before making the wreath. If you have the time to plan in advance, make the wreath base as much as a year before the wedding and store it until you are ready to decorate.

This wreath is not meant to be long lasting. Keep it out of direct sunlight. Cool weather will prolong the life of the fresh material, but orchids are tropical and do not appreciate frost. I made this in April in Pennsylvania, and it looked fresh for five days, when the Baker fern started to wilt and the asparagus fern began to drop its needles.

The orchids in their tubes still looked so fresh that I dried them in silica gel to make a future appearance on a gift wreath for the bride.

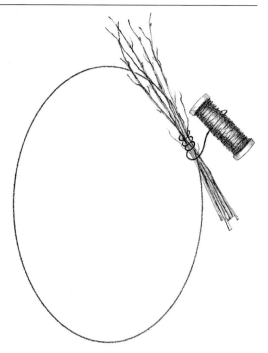

3. Starting at the top of the oval, lay the bottom half of one twig bunch along the wire frame and wrap tightly with the spool wire, as shown on the right. Take another bunch, lay it on top of the wrapped section of the first bunch, and wrap with wire. Continue down one side of the oval to the bottom, using five bunches in all and covering the wrapped sections of the previous bunches with the new twigs. As you come to the bottom, you may have to shorten the twigs if you are making a narrow oval like the one shown here. At the bottom, tie off and cut the wire.

4. Now start at the top on the other side of the wreath, repeating Step 3. Note that at the top of the wreath the twigs will meet each other in a cathedral point; there will be a patch of wrapped wire that is not covered with twigs but should be all but invisible.

5. Make a bow with the ribbon and wire it to the bottom of the wreath. Here, since I used three different kinds of ribbon, I laid them on top of each other and made the bow all at once. (See "Making a Bow" on page 243 for instructions.)

6. Add water to the orchid tubes if necessary to fill them. Stick the tubes in among the branches, three on each side, and wire them to the wreath with pieces of spool wire for extra security, if desired.

7. Add pieces of the two kinds of fern around the wreath. They will help hide the tubes. Either place the stems of the fern in the tubes with the orchids, or just stick them among the twigs, out of the water.

# Hair Wreaths for a Wedding

The bride's hair wreath is lavish with delicate dried flowers and herbs. The flower girl's, while using the same color theme, is as sturdy as possible, so little fingers won't ruin it before the ceremony. These designs work as well for prom queens and sweet sixteens, and for other special occasions.

## What You Need for the Bride

Dried flowers and herbs in the color theme of the wedding (Here I used globe amaranth, sweet Annie, lavender, larkspur, roundleaf oregano, winged everlasting, bells-of-Ireland, and tiny rosebuds.)

18-gauge wire
White floral tape
20- to 22-gauge floral spool wire
1¼ yards of 1-inch-wide ribbon
Clippers
Scissors
Wire cutters
Hot glue gun and glue sticks

## What You Do

1.  With the bride, decide where she will wear the wreath, that is, either low on the forehead, tipped back on the crown, or in another position. Measure the bride's head with the 18-gauge wire. Cut the wire 3 inches longer than measured.

2.  Wrap the wire with floral tape, completely covering the wire. Form the wire into a circle and bind the ends together, using up the extra three inches of wire.

3.  Cut the stems of the flowers and herbs 3 to 4 inches long. (Little pieces with no stems will be glued on at the end.)

4.  Tie the spool wire to the wreath. Form a small bundle of flowers in your fingers, perhaps two pieces of sweet Annie and one each of lavender, larkspur, and globe amaranth. Using the spool wire, tie the bundle to the wreath.

5.  Make another small bundle, using the same mixture of flowers or a different one. Place it over the stems of the first bundle and tie it in place. This wreath

used 14 bundles of flowers; each with sweet Annie and several other flowers. Glue on the rest of the flowers, filling in any bare spots.

6.  Make a bow with the ribbon. (See "Making a Bow" on page 243 for instructions.) Glue it to the wreath over the stems of the last bundle.

## What You Need for the Flower Girl

Sturdy dried flowers and leaves, like German statice, strawflowers, globe amaranth, and tiny rosebuds
1 plastic headband
1 yard of wire-edged ribbon to cover the headband
24 inches of ribbon for streamers
Clippers
Scissors
Hot glue gun and glue sticks

## What You Do

1.  Turn the ends of the wire-edged ribbon under. Secure with a drop of glue. Glue the ribbon to the headband, shirring as you go. The finished ribbon will look ruffled rather than flat.

2.  Glue on the dried leaves first, then the German statice, the strawflowers, and the smaller pieces.

3.  Cut the 24-inch length of ribbon into two 12-inch-long pieces. Glue the two pieces to the ends of the headband on the inside. These may be left as hanging tendrils or tied in a bow after placing the headband on the flower girl's head.

---

### ELLEN'S EXTRAS

USE THE FOLLOWING METHODS FOR DRYING THE MOST POPULAR WEDDING FLOWERS:

AIR-DRY BY HANGING: BABY'S-BREATH, HEATHERS, LARKSPUR, ROSES, WAX FLOWERS

DRY FLAT ON A SCREEN: QUEEN-ANNE'S-LACE

DRY IN SILICA GEL: CARNATIONS, LILIES, MUMS, ORCHIDS, SPRING BULB FLOWERS LIKE TULIPS

PRESS: FERNS AND LEAVES INCLUDING THOSE FROM ROSES AND OTHER FOLIAGE

---

# A Wedding Preserved

There are often precious few flowers left after a wedding to dry for future enjoyment. Here I've dried the orchids from the "Welcoming the Bride" wreath on page 98; a few somewhat wilted roses and Baker fern from a bridesmaid's bouquet; and the tulips and Queen-Anne's-lace from the head-table decoration.

## What You Need

Flower arrangement from the wedding
6 stems of preserved fern, like asparagus fern
Vine wreath base
Sealing spray for dried flowers
1 ribbon bow from the wedding
Clippers
Hot glue gun and glue sticks

## What You Do

1. Make an oval vine wreath base according to the instructions in "Welcoming the Bride" on page 98.

2. Take apart the arrangement you have to work with and discard any damaged or brown pieces. Keep the ribbon.

3. Decide which flowers you will air-dry, press, or dry in silica gel. Here I've replaced the fresh asparagus fern with purchased preserved fern. If you use preserved fern, cut it into pieces and glue them around the wreath. After all the other flowers are dried, glue them around the wreath base.

4. After the wreath is complete, spray the flowers that have been dried in silica

with three light coats of sealing spray, according to the package directions.

5. Hang this wreath out of direct sunlight. Humidity eventually fades all dried flowers and will quickly wilt all flowers dried in silica gel unless they are sealed.

# A Miser's Wreath

Lunaria has more common names than any other plant I know. I grew up calling it honesty. But most of its other names have to do with money: silver dollar plant, money plant, and pennies from heaven. Here is a wreath appropriate for a silver anniversary, to celebrate a financial transaction, or to tease a spendthrift.

## What You Need

10 well-branched stems of fresh silver dollar plant
14-inch-diameter straw wreath base
5 yards of gold ribbon, 2 to 3 inches wide
15 floral pins
3 yards of silver cording
Floral spool wire
Silver or aluminum spray paint
3 to 5 sand dollars (optional)
Clippers
Scissors
Wire cutters
Hot glue gun and glue sticks

## What You Do

1. Wrap the straw wreath base with the gold ribbon, overlapping the ribbon to cover the straw completely. Pin at each end with floral pins to secure.

### ELLEN'S EXTRAS

PICK SILVER DOLLAR PLANTS EARLY IN THE SUMMER, JUST AFTER THE PODS TURN BEIGE, AND HANG THEM INDOORS TO DRY. WHEN YOU ARE READY TO USE THEM, PEEL SOME TO EXPOSE THE TRANSLUCENT WHITE MEMBRANE WITHIN, AND LEAVE SOME UNPEELED SO YOU CAN SPRAY THEM SILVER.

2. Wrap the wreath with the cording, as shown below, then tie, leaving the ends about 6 inches long. Cut the cord and knot the ends so they won't unravel. Form the leftover cord into loops. Wire the loops onto the wreath where the other cording is tied.

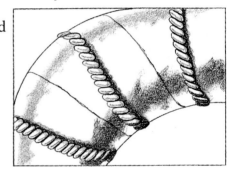

3. Spray half of the silver dollar pods with silver paint and let dry. Then cut all the silver dollar plant stems into lengths about 8 inches long.

4. Take small clusters of stems and pin them to the wreath with the floral pins, starting below the cording loops. Continue around the wreath, pinning additional clusters and hiding the stems of the previous clusters.

5. Wire on the sand dollars, if desired. They have natural holes through which you can string the wire. Glue on additional stems anywhere the silver dollar plant seems a little bare.

# Hit the High Notes

*I*n this musical pun, I used drumsticks and violas (pansies) as part of the decoration. Admirers will see a Victorian-style wreath with a musical theme, but a true gardener will understand the botanical joke.

## What You Need

Assortment of dried leaves and flowers (Here I used lemonleaf [salal], blue hydrangea, golden cockscomb, yarrow, bright star, drumstick flower, pansies, bunny-tail, and a grass *[Stipa pennata]*.)
Lid of an old peach basket or cheese box
4 sheets of old music
2 to 3 yards of musical-motif wire-edged ribbon
Floral tape
Clippers
Scissors
Hot glue gun and glue sticks
Utility knife or razor blade

## What You Do

1. Glue the four sheets of music all around the inside of the wooden lid, overlapping as necessary to cover the lid. Trim the sheets of music around the circumference using the utility knife or razor blade.

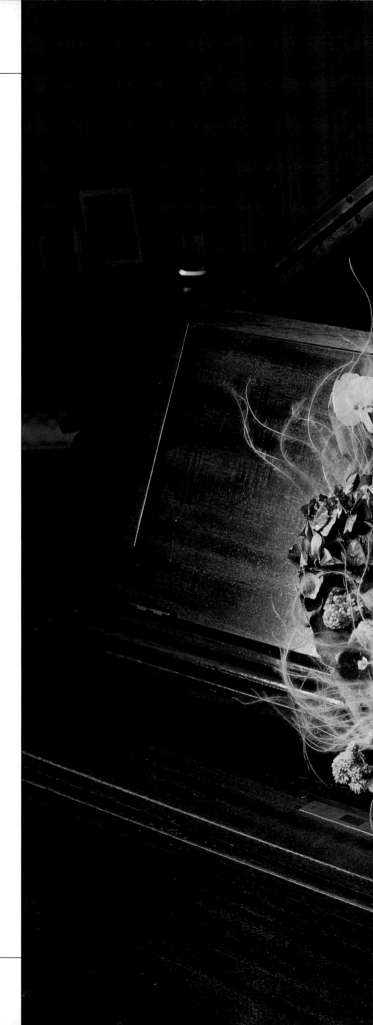

2. Make a bow with the ribbon and glue it to one side of the wreath, as shown in the photo on page 107. (See "Making a Bow" on page 243 for instructions.)

3. Lay a ring of leaves around the edge of the lid and glue them in place. Next, glue on the largest flowers—here the hydrangea—then glue on the golden cockscomb and yarrow.

4. Glue the drumstick flower in two clusters on each side of the bow. Now add the smaller flowers, ending with the pansies, which are fragile.

5. Bunch the grass in small clusters and wrap the stems with floral tape. Glue the clusters to the wreath.

## WREATHMAKER'S ❧WISDOM❧

*Although the flowers follow the round shape of the peach box lid in this project, I have allowed some to drift over the edges and into the middle to encourage a relaxed and romantic mood.*

*Substitute dried flowers freely, depending on the varieties you have available and the desired color combinations.*

*This ribbon was the perfect pattern, but the stark white and black was too contemporary looking for a Victorian-style wreath. I immersed the ribbon in a strong infusion of regular tea for about two hours, then dried and ironed it before making the bow. Tea-dyeing is an old technique for treating material to make it look antique.*

# work and Play

Small dolls make charming wreath ornaments. These Guatemalan farmers have just finished working in the fields as the children play. Dress old-fashioned clothespins with scraps of cloth for a similar effect.

## what You Need

Dried corn stalk, river cane, or bamboo shoot totaling 54 inches

Corn-leaf wreath on a straw base (See "Corn-Leaves Oval" on page 216 for instructions.)

About 70 stems of green wheat

About 20 stems of dried corn tassel, broomcorn, or sorghum

Decorative corns, like strawberry corn (optional)

Small dolls

12 strands of natural raffia

15 to 20 floral pins

Clippers

Scissors

Hot glue gun and glue sticks

## what You Do

1. To make the ladder, cut two pieces of stalk, each 17 inches long, and five pieces, each 4 inches long. Glue the 4-inch rungs to the 17-inch uprights.

2. Glue some of the dolls to the ladder in various poses, as shown in the photo.

3. Attach the ladder by tying the top and bottom to the wreath with raffia. Bring the raffia all the way around to the back of the wreath, tie, and cut off the ends.

4. Pin, tie, or glue the other dolls around the wreath. These dolls have legs under their clothing, and they can be secured to the base with floral pins.

5. Separate the green wheat into seven bundles of ten stems each. Tie each bundle with raffia. Tie or pin on the tassel near the bottom of the wreath, opposite the ladder. Then pin on the bundles of wheat around the wreath. Pin on the decorative corns, if desired.

# You Are What You Eat, Part I

*T*reasured koalas, discarded with childhood and hoarded by Mother with other valuables, reappear years later on, of all things, a wreath!

## What You Need

2 stems of preserved roundleaf eucalyptus

2 stems of fresh eucalyptus berry stems (available from florists)

18- to 20-inch-diameter kiwi vine wreath base

Stuffed toy koala bears

Floral spool wire

Clippers

Wire cutters

## What You Do

1. Make the kiwi vine wreath base. (See "Woven Vine" or "Wrapped Vine" on page 234 for instructions.)

2. The kiwi vine has so many loops and swirls, you should be able to find perching spots for the bears. Loop a wire around each bear's neck, tying it to a convenient branch. (The koala in the photo with his back turned is ashamed to show that his eyes and nose are missing, having been sacrificed to years of boy-handling.)

3. Cut side branches off the preserved eucalyptus stems. Stick the stems and side branches among the kiwi vine, tucking them beneath the wrapping wire that holds the wreath together.

4. Cut short lengths of eucalyptus berry stems, stripping off the fresh leaves if necessary. Tuck the berry stems around the wreath, slipping them under wires that are already there.

## WREATHMAKER'S WISDOM

The idea behind this wreath is to remove treasures from the cartons where they are stored and find a way to display them for your amusement. In our household, one child favored koalas. I chose kiwi vine as the base to emphasize the Australian theme, and eucalyptus because it's the real-life bears' preferred food.

In your household, what childhood treasures have you been hiding? Some doll or toy of yours perhaps? Get it out, select an appropriate wreath base, and search for natural materials that fit the theme or create a pun. Have Barbies? Decorate with barberries and lady's-mantle. Have Matchbox cars and trucks? Wire them through the windows, from the axles, and around the bumpers to a tough-looking vine wreath and add a little boxwood. I can hear the groans!

# You Are What You Eat, Part II

*P*andas and bamboo—perfect together. The larkspur is added simply to highlight the whiteness of the fur, not for the panda's diet.

## What You Need

16 pieces of fresh or dried bamboo, each 16 inches long and the diameter of your little finger
6 pieces of dried bamboo leaves
8 stems of dried white larkspur
8 rubber bands
9 strands of natural raffia
Floral spool wire
1 stuffed toy panda bear
Clippers
Scissors
Wire cutters
2 hooks for hanging

## What You Do

1. Separate the bamboo into four bundles of four pieces each. Working with the first bundle, wrap a rubber band 2 inches from each end of the bundle. Repeat for the remaining three bundles.

2. To make the wreath frame, lay out the four bundles in a square and wrap each corner in an X with two strands of raffia. Tie the raffia in the back and cut the ends short.

3. Slip two stems of bamboo leaves and three stems of larkspur under the raffia ties at the two bottom corners of the wreath frame. If necessary, tie the stems with a small piece of spool wire partway up the bamboo frame to hold the stems upright.

4. Sit the panda on the bottom of the wreath and tie it around the neck with a piece of spool wire to keep it in place.

5. Make a little bundle of the remaining larkspur and bamboo leaves and tie it together with a half piece of raffia. Use the other half of the raffia to tie the bundle to the panda's hand.

6. The panda's weight will tilt this wreath to one side, so be sure to hang the wreath from two hooks for balance.

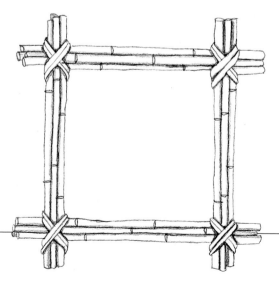

# The Wilds of Pennsylvania

The roadside crews come to our countryside and mow down wide swaths of wildflowers and grasses. I consider any roadside beauties to be free pickings and try to stay a step ahead of the mowers.

## What You Need

Bunches of air-dried of wildflowers and berries (Where I live, Joe-Pye weed is plentiful, so I used that freely; also included here are black-eyed Susans, ironweed, wild black raspberries, staghorn sumac, goldenrod, butterfly weed, yarrow, viper's bugloss, and peppergrass.)
18-inch-diameter straw wreath base
30 to 50 floral pins
Clippers

### ELLEN'S EXTRAS

I'M STRINGENT ABOUT AVOIDING PROTECTED SPECIES AND CAREFUL TO TAKE ONLY A SMALL PERCENTAGE OF THE FLOWERS GROWING IN ONE AREA. IN A FEW STATES IT'S ILLEGAL TO PICK WILDFLOWERS ON PUBLIC LAND, AND YOU SHOULD MAKE YOURSELF AWARE OF THE REGULATIONS BOTH WHERE YOU LIVE AND WHERE YOU TRAVEL. OF COURSE, YOU SHOULD NEVER TRESPASS ON PRIVATE PROPERTY WITHOUT THE PERMISSION OF THE OWNER.

## What You Do

1. Lay out a design in advance. Here I alternated clusters of Joe-Pye weed with clusters of the other materials. The sumac was used sparingly as an accent.

2. Cut the stems of your wildflowers and berries to 8 to 10 inches. Make small clusters of materials, either mixed or all one kind.

3. Pin the first cluster to the wreath base. Pin the next cluster over the stems of the first and continue around the wreath following the pattern you laid out.

# Birds of a Feather

*O*ne of the many ways to decorate the simple house shape on page 204 is to make it into a fanciful birdhouse. Gather fallen, brown pine needles for the nesting material.

## What You Need

50 stems of dried grass or grain (Here I used a mixture of wheat and oats.)
1 large handful of brown pine needles
Assorted pieces of small dried flowers
House-shaped, bark wreath base
1 extra piece of bark, 8 inches long
4-inch-long twig
2 artificial birds
Several small plastic eggs (optional)
3 small feathers (optional)
Clippers
Hot glue gun and glue sticks
White craft glue
Small bowl
Water
Muffin tin

## What You Do

1. Make the house-shaped wreath base. (See "Bark House and Woodland Initial" on page 204 for instructions.)

2. Cut the stems of the grasses to 2 inches below the seed head. To thatch the roof, start at the roof peak and glue grasses down both sides of the roof, pointing the stems downward. Trim the stems of the bottom pieces as necessary.

3. To make the nest, mix ¼ cup of white glue and ¼ cup of water in the bowl. Dump in the pine needles. Mix until the pine needles are coated.

4. Put the pine needles in a cup of the muffin tin and form a nest shape with your fingers. Allow to dry, then carefully remove the nest from the cup and glue it on the house.

5. Glue the flowers to the back of the wreath at the bottom, so they peek up from the inside about 2 inches, as shown in the photo.

6. Glue the extra bark piece so it extends from the house like a gangplank.

7. Glue the twig in place for a perch and glue on the birds. Glue on feathers near the birds, if desired.

# An A-Social Butterfly

This butterfly flits by itself and alights wherever you need a spot of color. Enjoy making a fanciful pattern with colorful flowers and let your spirits soar.

## What You Need

Assortment of dried flowers and grasses, whatever you have available in a bright and pleasing color combination—this project uses lots of flowers because of the compact style, so start with something plentiful (Here I've used strawflowers, roses, bunny-tail, safflower, globe amaranth, cockscomb, and bright star.)

1 stick, 8 inches long and the thickness of your index finger

Old newspaper

18-inch square of corrugated cardboard, cut from a carton

2 feet of thin corrugated cardboard, cut from a roll (available from packaging supply stores)

Heavy-duty scissors or clippers

Wire cutters

Utility knife

Hot glue gun and glue sticks

Ruler

Pencil

2 picture hooks with tape attachment

Picture wire

## What You Do

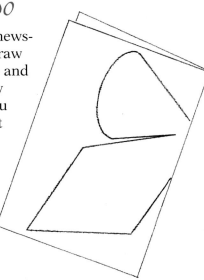

1. Fold a sheet of newspaper in half. Draw the shape of top and bottom butterfly wings. When you are satisfied, cut out and open the paper. You will have a perfectly symmetrical butterfly.

2. Lay the pattern on the thick square of cardboard and trace around the outside. Cut it out. The wings will probably separate from each other at this point. That's all right.

3. From the thin corrugated cardboard roll, cut strips 4 inches wide and long enough to outline the outside of each wing. This flexible cardboard forms the "edges" of the wreath.

4. Turn the strips to their smooth sides and score down the middle of each strip with the utility knife, using the ruler as a guide. This will make it easier to fold the strip.

5. Fold the strip in half lengthwise. Add a drop of glue inside the folded areas to help the cardboard remain folded. With the folded edge up, glue the strips all around each wing.

6. Glue the four wings together in the center, holding them in place until the glue dries. Glue the wings to the stick, using the photo as a guide.

7. Cut two 10 × 1-inch cardboard strips from the roll. Curl them tightly around a pencil. Remove the pencil and glue one end of each strip to the top of the stick to make the antennae.

8. Decide on a floral pattern using the materials and colors you have handy. Cut all of your chosen flowers short and glue them in place. Decorate the wings in pairs. The top wings should be identical and the bottom wings should be identical.

9. Use the picture hooks with tape attachments to hang the wreath. Stick the hooks to the back of the top pair of wings, one on each side. Run a wire between them and hang like a picture.

# Proud as a Peacock

*L*uminescent peacock feathers have been used to trim luxurious capes, hats, fans, and flower arrangements. In this wreath, they need little decoration to emphasize their beauty.

## What You Need

5 branches of fresh tree trimmings, like birch, with 3 branches each 4 feet long and 2 branches each 3 feet long
Floral spool wire
Copper spray paint
1½ yards of luminescent ribbon (Here I combined two different colors, using 1½ yards of each.)
6 peacock feathers
Clippers
Scissors
Wire cutters
Hot glue gun and glue sticks

## What You Do

1. Make the wreath base by taking the two 3-foot-long branches and holding them near the bottom with one hand. Bring the top of the branches around and down to form an oval that measures 9 inches high. Let the remaining branch lengths swing out to the side, as shown in the illustration on page 120.

# Grasshoppers at Play

*I*deas for designs spring from sundry sources. I knew I needed to design a grasshopper wreath as soon as I saw these clever imitations and started to think of where they would be happiest playing. As in nature, they are partially camouflaged by the colors of their environment.

## What You Need

8 strips of birch bark or other bark
Dried grasses or herbs (Here I used 20 stems of swamp grass, 2 stems of lady's-mantle, and 3 stems of penny-cress.)
2 sheets of decorative gift-wrap paper in a natural pattern
12-inch-diameter wire box frame
12 inches of twine
3 artificial grasshoppers
Clippers
Hot glue gun and glue sticks
1 cup of thick white craft glue
Bowl
¼ cup of water

### ELLEN'S EXTRAS

USE THIS SAME PAPIER-MÂCHÉ TECHNIQUE TO MAKE WREATH FRAMES FOR SPECIAL OCCASIONS. SELECT HOLIDAY, BIRTHDAY, OR PERIOD GIFT-WRAP PAPER, AND FOLLOW STEPS 1 THROUGH 4 ON THE RIGHT. DECORATE WITH APPROPRIATE FLOWERS, HERBS, PODS, OR FOLIAGE.

## What You Do

1. Tear the paper lengthwise into rough strips about 6 inches wide.

2. Mix the white glue and the water in a bowl. Crumple up the paper strips and thoroughly coat them with the glue mixture.

3. Remove the strips from the bowl, squeezing off the excess glue, and wrap loosely around the wire frame to cover. Keep wrapping the strips of paper around the frame, building up the thickness of the wreath until you've used up all the paper. Let the paper dry thoroughly, about one to two days.

4. Hot-glue the strips of birch bark around the wreath.

5. Tie the bundle of swamp grass with about 6 inches of twine and hot-glue it to the back of the wreath at the bottom center. Tie the other grasses into a shorter bundle with the rest of the twine and hot-glue it to the front of the wreath at the bottom center.

6. Glue on the grasshoppers with hot glue wherever they cavort naturally.

# Summers at the Shore

*T*hese are my memories of summer. Postcards from my childhood era are the starting point for this wreath. I began with girlhood memories of walks on the beach, gathering shells, and the scent of summer lawns bordered by hydrangeas. I added postcards from that era to create this summer wreath.

## What You Need

12 to 20 stems of dried blue and lavender-pink hydrangeas (The number depends on the size of the flower heads.)
18-inch-diameter straw wreath base
20 floral pins
5 old postcards
3 starfish
9 to 15 seashells
5-inch-long floral picks without wires for each shell and starfish
Clippers
Hot glue gun and glue sticks

## What You Do

1. Starting anywhere on the wreath base, pin 2 to 3 stems of hydrangea in a bundle to the base with floral pins. If the hydrangea is too large or sticks out too much in one place, trim off small clusters of flowers and set aside.

2. Glue one postcard to the wreath base, nestling it under the hydrangea.

3. Pin another cluster of hydrangea to the wreath base on each side of the postcard and behind it, if necessary. Then glue another postcard onto the base.

4. Continue around the wreath, spacing the postcards at approximately equal intervals and filling in between them with hydrangeas.

5. Glue a pick to the back of each starfish and seashell. When the glue is dry, insert the picks into the wreath, hiding the picks in the flowers, but making sure the decorations are visible.

6. Glue any set-aside flower clusters onto the base to fill bare spots.

CHAPTER 5

# Holiday Wreaths

IF YOU DECORATE FOR CHRISTMAS, A
FRONT-DOOR WREATH OF NATURAL
MATERIALS IS ESSENTIAL. IT DELIGHTS
THE EYE OF EVERY PASSERBY, WELCOMES
GUESTS WITH WARMTH, AND WAFTS A
FRESH SCENT INTO THE HOUSE WITH THE
ENTRANCE OF EACH FAMILY MEMBER.
FOR ALL HOLIDAYS, BOTH INTERIOR AND
EXTERIOR WREATHS GRACE HOME AND
WORK SPACES. CREATE DESIGNS TO FIT
THE OCCASION IN INEXPENSIVE YET
UNUSUAL WAYS.

# You Hold the Key to My Heart

*E*xploit the crimson color of red-twig dogwood in winter to make a Valentine's Day wreath. Appropriate for a protected front door or anywhere inside, this wreath displays part of my key collection.

## What You Need

13 pliable branches of red-twig dogwood, each 28 to 30 inches long
15 sprigs of baby's-breath
Floral spool wire
Old keys
Monofilament fishing line (optional)
Clippers
Wire cutters
Hot glue gun and glue sticks

## What You Do

1. To make the heart, hold four branches at their stems in one hand. With the other hand, bend the tips down and grasp together with the stems, forming a teardrop shape. Bind together with spool wire. Take four more branches and repeat.

2. Now bind the two sides of the heart together with spool wire at the top and bottom.

3. Take the remaining five branches and lay them vertically along the center of the heart. With spool wire, bind them to the heart at the bottom and where the curves start.

4. Tuck in or clip off any stray twigs, but leave some for hanging the keys.

5. Glue the sprigs of baby's-breath around the heart and up the center, hiding the wire.

6. Hang the wreath in place, either upright or tilted, then either hang the keys from little twigs or attach them with small pieces of spool wire or fishing line, if desired.

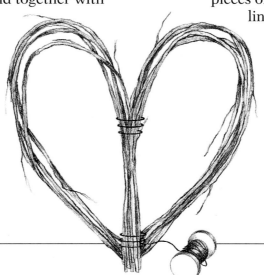

# Hearts and Flowers

*H*earts are a decorative motif in the folk art and traditions of many cultures. They have been carved, woven, painted, embroidered, glazed, and stitched. Here are two hearts together, made as one— what could be more appropriate for Valentine's Day?

## What You Need

6 large handfuls of fresh or dried Spanish moss (You can purchase fresh from a florist and dried from most craft shops.)

Assortment of dried flowers, leaves, and berries with very short stems (Here I used strawflowers, cockscomb, German statice, colored statice, larkspur, love-in-a-mist, eucalyptus, and pepperberries.)

1 sheet of newspaper

Corrugated cardboard, cut from a carton

2 floral pins

Thin floral spool wire or very fine gold twine

Clippers

Scissors

Wire cutters

Hot glue gun and glue sticks

Pencil

## What You Do

1. Fold the sheet of newspaper in half and draw one side of a heart on it. My hearts are long and narrow, but you can make yours more plump if you prefer. When you are satisfied, cut out the pattern. Open the newspaper sheet to check and adjust as necessary, keeping both sides identical. Now cut out the center, leaving a 1½-inch-wide heart-shaped "frame" of paper. This is your pattern.

2. Trace two hearts from this pattern onto the cardboard and cut them out.

3. Turn the cardboard hearts sideways, overlapping the points of the two hearts by about 6 inches. Glue the hearts together.

4. Decide which way you will hang the wreath, horizontally, as shown in the photo on the opposite page, or vertically. Use two hangers for balance. To make a hanger, insert a floral pin ½ inch from the top edge on each side of the top of the wreath and bend up. (See "How to Hang a Wreath" on page 240 for instructions.)

5. Cover the front of the wreath with Spanish moss. Glue it to the top and edges. If you have enough moss, pile on more all around the face of the wreath and wrap it in place with the spool wire or fine twine.

6. Glue the dried flowers directly into the moss. Here the flowers were spread somewhat evenly around the surface of the wreath. Choose any pattern you wish.

## WREATHMAKER'S WISDOM

*Fresh Spanish moss is a lovely, pale greenish gray and will not crumble as you work with it. It will dry in place. Dry Spanish moss, if old, will be very crumbly, and you will waste a lot making your crafts. Moss newly dried (within six months), if sprayed with water and left to sit for half an hour, will rehydrate, get back some color, and won't crumble as you work with it.*

# Easter Centerpiece

*M*ost of the flowers in this table wreath will dry if left in place; see "Easter Centerpiece Redux" on page 29 for the dried version of this wreath. Moss-covered bunnies add a lighthearted note to this more formal fresh-flower centerpiece.

## What You Need

**For the fresh centerpiece:**
Assortment of fresh flowers and leaves
Fresh-flower food (optional)
12- to 14-inch-diameter Oasis foam ring
Platter or large dinner plate
Clippers
Bucket of water

**For the bunnies:**
Green sheet moss
Tiny buds from pussy willow
Bunny-tail grass
Plant mister with water
1 bunny made of papier-mâché or
    ceramic (It can be old, cracked,
    painted, or unpainted.)
Clippers
Hot glue gun and glue sticks

## What You Do

1. Condition the fresh flowers by recutting the stems, removing the bottom leaves, and letting them stand in a bucket of water for at least six hours or overnight. Add fresh-flower food according to the package directions, if desired.

2. Soak the Oasis ring in water for thirty minutes. Remove, let drain, and wipe the bottom. Place on a platter or plate.

3. Here the flowers are primarily in Easter colors of gold and lavender. Leaves, such as boxwood, form a circle around the bottom of the ring and help hide the base. Mix flowers from the florist with flowers from the garden, like forsythia or azalea, if you have them.

4. Insert the largest flowers, such as the lilies, first. Cut the stems short on leaves and flowers as you work with them. One stem of lilies will give you many blooms with which to work. Then add the smaller flowers. Add more greens at the end to fill in any bare spots.

5. To make the bunnies, mist the moss heavily with water to prevent crumbling as you work.

6. Dribble hot glue on the bunny form, working a section at a time. Press on the moss in that area. Keep adding glue and pressing on moss until the bunny is completely covered.

7. Add three small pussy willow buds for the nose and mouth, and glue on some bunny-tail grass for the tail.

# stars and stripes

*O*n this wreath the plant material is the accent rather than the featured performer. Bare twigs, sprayed white, burst out from the red, white, and blue like firecrackers in celebration.

## What You Need

- 4 to 6 bare twig branches, each 15 inches long
- 16-inch-diameter straw wreath base
- Flat white spray paint
- 5 yards of white paper ribbon
- 30 to 50 straight pins
- 6 yards of 2-inch-wide navy ribbon
- 4 yards of light blue cording
- 3 yards of red cording
- 10 to 12 gold stars (Here I used metal.)
- Clippers
- Scissors
- Hot glue gun and glue sticks

## What You Do

1. Spray the twigs with the white paint and set aside to dry. Untwist the white paper ribbon, if it is twisted, then wrap the wreath base with the paper ribbon to cover. Stick the pins through the ribbon into the wreath base to hold both ends, and in the middle if you need extra security.

2. Wrap the navy ribbon around the wreath, letting some stripes of white show. Again, pin the ribbon to the wreath to secure.

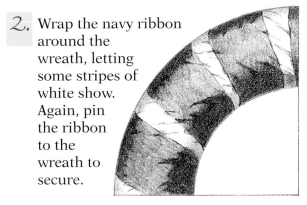

3. Knot the ends of the red cording and the blue cording to prevent unraveling. Fold the length of blue cording in half. Leave about 12 inches dangling at the bottom and drape the cording loosely around the wreath, pushing straight

### ELLEN'S EXTRAS

TO KEEP THE COST DOWN WHEN MAKING THIS WREATH, SUBSTITUTE TWISTED PAPER RIBBON IN RED AND LIGHT BLUE IN PLACE OF THE CORDING. USE THE PAPER RIBBON, STILL TWISTED, FOR THE DRAPE. OR GET MORE FOR YOUR MONEY FROM THE CORDING BY USING IT FOR DIFFERENT SEASONS OF THE YEAR. SEE THE PHOTO FOR THE "TRADITIONAL EVERGREENS" WREATH ON PAGE 156 FOR USE OF A SIMILAR CORDING ON A CHRISTMAS WREATH.

pins in to hold it in place. When you get all around, make one or two loops at the bottom and pin to hold.

4. Drape the red cording around the wreath in a similar fashion, but without doubling it. Use pins to secure it to the wreath.

5. Pin or glue the stars to the wreath. Here some of the stars have little holes through which to insert the pins while others do not.

6. Glue the twig branches to the wreath near the looped cording "bow," extending them out like a star burst.

# Mask Wreath

*M*asks have been created for dances, ceremonies, and entertainment throughout history. Make your own history with this simple wreath featuring bright yellow masks.

## What You Need

12 reasonably straight twigs, each 18 to
   22 inches long
12 preserved yellow oak leaves
8 pressed red oak leaves (optional)
9 sprigs of dried tansy or small yarrow heads
10 to 12 dried yellow strawflower heads
4 dried gloriosa daisies, black-eyed
   Susans, or sunflowers
14 stems of dried purple larkspur (optional)
Floral spool wire
2 purchased Halloween masks
Clippers
Scissors
Wire cutters
Hot glue gun and glue sticks

## What You Do

1. Gather the twigs in four piles of three twigs each. Take the four piles and form a rough square or rectangle that is 10 inches across at the center, with the twigs sticking out at each corner. Tie the twigs with spool wire at each intersection.

2. Cut the strings off the masks. Glue the masks at opposite corners of the wreath, facing each other.

3. In the mask corners, glue on three yellow leaves and one red leaf in each corner, if desired.

4. Glue on three sprigs of tansy, two or three strawflower heads, a gloriosa daisy, and four stems of purple larkspur for a surprising color contrast.

5. In the other two corners, glue on one gloriosa daisy and the remaining leaves, strawflowers, larkspur, and sprigs of tansy.

# Primitive Mask Wreath

Scare the goblins away from your door by working your magic on this mask. Children will love to assist you. Or, better yet, let them create their own.

## What You Need

Assortment of dried materials, particularly different-shaped flowers (Here I used tall, spiked ones like plumed celosia, pitcher plant,* and rat-tail statice. I also used round shapes like strawflowers, globe amaranths, poppy pods, green hops, and silver dollar plant pods.)

7 × 9-inch piece of green sheet moss (doesn't need to be in one piece)

9-inch-diameter heavy paper plate, like Chinet

Black spray paint

12-inch length of picture wire

1 purchased black mask

Clippers

Wire cutters

Hot glue gun and glue sticks

*NOTE: Pitcher plants are endangered and should not be collected from the wild. If you don't grow your own, make sure that your floral supplier is selling you propagated, not wild-collected, plants.*

## What You Do

1. Turn the plate over to the "wrong" side. Spray with black paint. Let dry. This will now be the "right" side.

2. Poke two tiny holes ½ inch from the edge of the plate and opposite each

other. Run the wire through each hole and wrap like a picture wire. The mask is now ready to hang when completed.

3. Glue the sheet moss to the black side of the plate, covering the lower two-thirds of the plate. Glue the mask to the moss. Make a "headdress" by gluing the spiked materials to the plate above the mask, as shown in the photo.

4. Using the remaining materials, glue on the eyes, mouth, and other creative features—the more elaborate the better. Here I was aiming for glamorous; you can try scary or comical.

# Halloween Wreath for Sophisticates

*If* you have children under ten, skip this project. For them, Halloween must be ghostly and gruesome. But if you don't need your pumpkins orange, and you value a Halloween decoration that will last through Christmas, try this gilded pumpkin wreath.

## What You Need

3 mini pumpkins
7 mini corns, preferably pink (See "Seed Sources" on page 246 for information on seed suppliers.)
10 stems of dried love-in-a-mist pods
9 stems of dried burgundy cockscomb
15-inch-diameter sturdy vine wreath base
Gold spray paint
Copper and moss green spray paints (optional)
Floral spool wire
Clippers
Wire cutters
Hot glue gun and glue sticks

## What You Do

1. Buy or make the vine wreath base. (See "Woven Vine" or "Wrapped Vine" on page 234 for instructions.)

2. Spray the pumpkins and three of the corns with gold paint. Let them dry.

3. If desired, lightly mist the wreath base with touches of green, gold, and copper spray paint.

4. Divide the love-in-a-mist into two five-stem bundles. Turn the bundles end to end and overlap 5 to 6 inches to make a swag. Bind with the spool wire and attach the swag to the wreath base with more wire.

5. Glue the three pumpkins to the vine wreath near the center of the swag. Hold them in place until the glue dries completely, about 15 seconds.

6. Next glue on the gold corn, then the pink corn in the positions shown in the photo on the opposite page.

7. Glue on the cockscomb last. Keep two stems as long as the love-in-a-mist, and shorten the other stems, cutting them to fill in any bare spots.

# Thanksgiving Wreath 'Round Cornucopia

Display the bountiful harvest in a different way. Instead of stuffing a cornucopia with fruits, fashion a lush dried wreath on the rim.

## What You Need

2 dried artichokes
6 dried pomegranates
6 mini pumpkins
3 stems of dried lemonleaf (salal)
4 mini corns
4 to 6 stems of dried hydrangea
9 clusters of red pepperberries, each 3 to 4 inches long, cut from 1 long stem
7 bright, dried flowers (Here I used heliopsis, but yellow strawflowers can be used.)
Papier-mâché, wicker, or similar cornucopia
Clippers
Hot glue gun and glue sticks

## What You Do

1. Glue all the heavy materials directly onto the rim of the cornucopia in this order: artichokes at the bottom, then pomegranates and pumpkins scattered around the rim. When you glue something heavy, be sure to hold it in place

# Traditional Evergreens

*I* look forward to making fresh evergreen wreaths as much for their sweet-pungent smell as for their natural appearance. All you need are some berried branches, conifers ranging from blue to yellow-green, and a few cones. Accent the red and green ribbons with cording and tassels.

## *What You Need*

48 to 60 cuttings of assorted evergreens,
each 4 to 8 inches long (You can use fir,
spruce, juniper, cedar, or others, as
many as possible with berries.)

3 conifer cones

12-inch-diameter wire wreath frame with
clamps

20- to 22-gauge floral spool wire

2 tassels

2 yards of colorful cording

3 yards of green ribbon

3 yards of red ribbon

Clippers

Scissors

Wire cutters

## *What You Do*

1.  Make the wreath base by clamping four
    or five evergreen cuttings in each
    clamp. Save the berried pieces and
    those with the most color for the top of
    each pile. Put the stems in the clamp
    and close each side as tightly as pos-
    sible. (See "Wire Wreath Frame with
    Clamps" on page 236 for instructions.)
    Clamp each bundle of four to five cut-
    tings so that they overlap and hide the
    stems of the previous bundle.

2.  Cut 10 inches of spool wire. Wrap the
    wire under the "petals" of each cone
    and twist. Tie the cones securely to the
    wreath base using the ends of the wire.

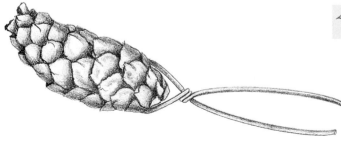

## WREATHMAKER'S ❧WISDOM❧

Nothing cheapens a fine wreath
faster than a cheap-looking ribbon. For
this wreath, where the ribbon and
cording are the only decoration, it pays
to use an excellent-quality ribbon. After
use you will be eager to undo the bows
and stash these beauties in your supply
cupboard to be reincarnated on some
other project.

When choosing fresh greens for this
project, try to get variations in color:
forest greens, blue-greens, and yellow-
greens. What you don't have yourself,
buy from local sources or beg a few cuttings from friends. As an alternative you
can buy a ready-made wreath, add several different greens to spruce it up,
then decorate as shown in the photo on
the opposite page.

3.  Knot the tassels to the two ends of
    the cording. Drape the cording from
    the wreath starting at the two o'clock
    position. Tie it in place with small
    pieces of spool wire secured to the
    branches.

4.  Make one bow from the red ribbon and
    one bow from the green ribbon. (See
    "Making a Bow" on page 243.) Nestle
    the green ribbon above the red and
    wire the two together; then wire the
    bows to the wreath.

# christmas Wreath Tree

*A* series of seven graduated straw wreaths quickly forms a charming tree. The decorations are reminiscent of wheat weaving without the intricacies of form. A volcano of black-bearded wheat erupts from the top of the tree.

## what You Need

125 stalks of black-bearded wheat
About 360 stalks of green wheat or other grain
20 to 30 teasels
About 24 dried poppy pods
30 to 40 dried red globe amaranths, rose hips, or sumac pieces, or a combination
7 straw wreath bases (with diameters of 18 inches, 16 inches, 14 inches, 12 inches, 10 inches, 8 inches, and 6 inches)
17-inch-diameter circle of corrugated cardboard, cut from a carton
Cake stand or jardiniere
Newspaper
1 bundle of red raffia
Straight pins
Clippers
Scissors
Hot glue gun and glue sticks

## what You Do

1. Place the circle of corrugated cardboard on top of the cake stand.

2. Using the cardboard as a base, stack the wreaths with the largest on the bottom and the smallest on top. You can glue them together with hot glue

### ELLEN'S EXTRAS

I WOULDN'T DREAM OF MAKING MY OWN STRAW WREATHS SINCE THEY'RE INEXPENSIVE AND EASY TO FIND IN ANY CRAFT STORE. THE STORE-BOUGHT VARIETY HAVE AN ADDITIONAL ADVANTAGE: MACHINES PACK THE STRAW MORE TIGHTLY THAN YOU CAN, ELIMINATING SOME MESS AND MAKING PIN INSERTIONS MORE SECURE.

HERE ARE SOME SUBSTITUTES FOR THIS PROJECT. INSTEAD OF WHEAT, USE OATS, BARLEY, FOXTAIL, OR ANY GRASS OR GRAIN THAT IS GREEN-BEIGE IN COLOR. INSTEAD OF RED ROSE HIPS, TRY RED PEPPERBERRIES. INSTEAD OF TEASEL USE SMALL PODS LIKE HEMLOCK OR LARCH, OR NUTS LIKE PECANS OR WALNUTS.

to make a permanent stack, but I prefer to leave them unsecured. That way, I can easily take the tree apart at the end of the holiday season and use the individual straw wreaths for other projects.

3. Stuff the center of the wreath stack with crumpled newspaper up to the 10-inch wreath. The paper will serve as a base for the sheaf of wheat to stand on, yet be invisible inside the tree.

4. With the raffia, tightly tie all the black-bearded wheat into a bundle, just under the seed heads. Push up some of the center stalks from the bottom to make the sheaf cone-shaped.

5. Insert the bundle into the tree. Cut the wheat stems and/or adjust the height of the newspaper so that the sheaf seems to burst out of the tree.

6. Cut the green wheat stems to 3 inches. Make small bundles of three to five stalks of green wheat tied with a small bow of raffia. The number of bundles depends on your preference and how many other decorations you want to use. Here I made 72 bundles.

7. Pin the bundles to the wreath by sticking a straight pin through the bow and directly into the straw. Use the smaller bundles toward the top of the wreath.

8. Add the teasels, rose hips, poppy pods, and globe amaranths as desired for tree "decorations." Pin or glue them to the tree, or merely insert their stems in the spaces between the wreaths.

# Holiday Squares

*H*olly berries grow on year-old wood, so they usually appear not at the tip, but 5 or 6 inches down the stem. A square wreath is the perfect way to show them off.

## What You Need

20 stems of fresh red-twig dogwood
8 stems of fresh blue atlas cedar
8 stems of fresh variegated holly
4 stems of fresh variegated lily-of-
the-valley bush
18- or 20-gauge floral spool wire
3 bells (optional)
Clippers
Wire cutters

## What You Do

1. Divide each of the plant materials into four equal piles, one to make each leg of the square. The red-twig dogwood and blue atlas cedar are the longest; the holly and lily-of-the-valley bush are shorter simply because that is what I had available. Adjust the sizes to your own materials.

2. Make each leg of the square separately. For each leg, use one pile from Step 1, with the cedar stems as the base and the shortest stems on top. Tie the spool wire near the top of the longest stem and wrap the wire securely down the pile, holding everything together. Tie off and cut the wire. Repeat to make the other three legs.

3. You will now have four separate sides. Put them together on the worktable so they form a square, with the tips of one side overlapping the ends of the other side by 4 to 5 inches.

4. Bind the intersection of the two piles at each corner with the spool wire. The branches form the only frame here, so the wreath looks delicate. For a sturdier frame, or to make a bigger square, use a length of 12-gauge wire under each pile of material as you are forming the legs. Wrap it together with the greens to make them more rigid.

5. If you are using bells or other decorations, tie them on with wire.

# Punched "Tin"

*U*sing fresh lemonleaf (salal) and some paint, you can achieve a fine representation of these classic Mexican ornamental tin designs.

## What You Need

65 to 75 fresh lemonleaf (salal) leaves
12 small dried red peppers
Ice pick, rounded toothpick, nail, or other "punching" tool
Newspaper
Silver spray paint
12 × 15-inch piece of corrugated cardboard, cut from a carton
1 mirror or picture frame (Here I used an 8 × 10-inch mirror.)
Clippers
Utility knife
Hot glue gun and glue sticks
2-inch-wide masking tape
Ruler

## What You Do

1. To get the "punched" look, poke holes with your ice pick in each fresh leaf. Poke them in any desired pattern, but use approximately the same pattern for all the leaves. Prepare more leaves than you need so you can pick and choose among the sizes as you are making your design. You can also keep some leaves unpunched for variety.

2. To make flat leaves, dry the leaves for one to two weeks between layers of newspaper that are placed under something heavy, such as stacks of books.

### ELLEN'S EXTRAS

FRESH LEMONLEAF (SALAL) LEAVES ARE STURDY, ROLL COMPLIANTLY, AND DRY IN POSITION. YOU CAN CUT THEM SMALLER, FRINGE THE EDGES, OR FORM DIFFERENT SHAPES. USE YOUR IMAGINATION TO CREATE OTHER LEAF DESIGNS, AS WELL AS OTHER POSSIBLE WREATH DESIGNS— ROUND, OVAL, OR EXOTIC. USE THE TECHNIQUE DESCRIBED HERE TO WREATHE IMPORTANT ANNOUNCEMENTS OR TO MAKE A WREATH IN THE TRADITIONAL OPEN-CENTERED FORM.

3. To make rolled leaves, cut off the top and bottom of each fresh leaf; roll like a cigarette. Secure with a dot of glue.

4. To make a fan, overlap the fresh leaves at the bottom and secure with glue.

5. Spread out the rolled and fanned leaves on your work surface and leave them at room temperature for one to two weeks.

6. When the leaves are all dry, spray them with the silver paint.

7. Snip about ½ inch off each corner of the cardboard rectangle. If you are using it to frame a mirror, measure the mirror and, with a utility knife, cut an

opening in the center of the cardboard
½ inch smaller than the size of the
mirror. Use this same technique for a
picture frame.

8. With the silver paint, spray the cardboard on the front, back, and edges.
Allow to dry.

9. When the paint is dry, tape the mirror
to the back of the cardboard.

10. Glue the leaves around the cardboard
frame in the pattern of your choice.
Start with the flat leaves, then add the
shaped leaves. Here the outer border of
leaves is slanted outward, and the inner
border points downward. There is a
different treatment at the top and
bottom center.

11. Glue the hot peppers inside or on top
of the leaf shapes as you wish.

# Sun, Moon, and Stars

$\mathcal{M}$y accumulation of celestial bodies is the starting point for this wreath. Among the sun, moon, and stars are buttons, beads, and tree ornaments.

## What You Need

30-inch-diameter wreath of fresh evergreens, like fir
6 dried sunflower heads
3½ yards of ribbon
Ornaments to complement your theme
Ornament hooks, thin wire, or monofilament fishing line
Clippers
Scissors
Hot glue gun and glue sticks

## What You Do

1. Buy or make an evergreen wreath base. (See "Wire Wreath Frame with Clamps" on page 236.)

2. Make a bow from 2 yards of the ribbon and tie the bow to the wreath. (See "Making a Bow" on page 243 for instructions.) Then wrap the remaining 1½ yards of ribbon around the wreath, tying it to the back of the wreath frame to hide the ends of the ribbon.

3. Hook or wire the ornaments to the greenery with small pieces of thin wire or fishing line. Glue the sunflower heads to the wreath with hot glue.

# Good Enough to Eat

*F*or a Christmas wreath, this one is slightly offbeat. Don't be surprised if the birds come to enjoy the berries.

## What You Need

Wreath of fresh greens, like boxwood
About 24 stems of red berries, like wild rose hips, holly, red pepperberries, or canella
9 dried sunflowers
1 ready-made bow with wire or 2 generous yards of red paper ribbon
5 to 7 small artificial cardinals or other birds
7 to 9 floral picks with wire, each 5 inches long
Green floral tape
Clippers

## What You Do

1. Attach the bow to the top of the wreath with wire or make a bow from the paper ribbon and tie it to the top of the wreath. (See "Making a Bow" on page 243.)

2. Affix the birds to the greens. Look for birds with little clips or wires attached to make this process easy.

3. Attach several stems of berries to a floral pick, then wrap with floral tape. Insert the pick deep in among the greens to hold it securely. Continue making small bunches of berries and adding them to the wreath until you are satisfied with the look.

4. Poke the sunflower stems into the greens to hold them securely.

# Ice and Snow

*I* love a Christmas wreath that says *winter* and can be left in place after the holidays are over. Construct this ice-and-snow wreath to enjoy from December to March.

## What You Need

12 stems of purchased preserved juniper, each 4 feet long

3 to 5 pinecones (misted with matte white paint, if desired)

8 to 10 small clusters of preserved bleached baby's-breath

12-inch-diameter wire wreath frame

Floral spool wire

2½ yards of fine white ribbon

7 white ball ornaments made of fuzzy cotton or pearlized glass

20 plastic icicles

Clippers

Scissors

Wire cutters

Hot glue gun and glue sticks

## What You Do

1. Cut the preserved juniper into pieces about 8 inches long. You will need about 60 to 70 cut pieces.

2. Tie the spool wire onto the frame. Make a bundle of five to six pieces of juniper, lay it on the frame, and bind tightly with the spool wire. For a very full wreath, place another bundle alongside the first and wrap it with the wire.

3. Make another bundle and lay it on the wreath, overlapping the stems of the first two bundles. Continue wiring on the juniper in bundles until the frame is covered. Tie off the wire.

4. Tie the ribbon into a bow and place it on the wreath at the one o'clock position. Let the ribbon tails intertwine with the branches. (See "Making a Bow" on page 243.)

5. Wrap pieces of wire around the cones between the bottom "petals" and wire them to the wreath near the bow. (See the illustration on page 157.)

6. Use small pieces of spool wire to tie the balls onto the juniper branches. Here all the balls are spread out over the top section of the wreath.

7. Position the icicles and wire them to the branches with little pieces of spool wire. The icicles should all hang vertically, as if gravity were pulling the icy water down.

8. Tuck in pieces of bleached baby's-breath where there are bare spots. Secure the pieces with glue.

## ELLEN'S EXTRAS

PURCHASE PRESERVED PLANT MATERIAL RATHER THAN TRY TO PRESERVE IT YOURSELF. MATERIAL IS ALMOST ALWAYS BLEACHED OR DYED DURING THE PROCESS OF PRESERVING IN GLYCERINE, AND IT TAKES A LOT OF EXPERIMENTATION AND MESS TO GET THE PROPORTIONS CORRECT.

# All That Glitters

This is one of the quickest, longest-lasting wreaths in this book, and one that will withstand assaults by the weather.

## What You Need

Assortment of dried leaves and pods
  (Here I used lemonleaf [salal] leaves
  and poppy, wheat, safflower, oriental
  nigella, and teasel pods.)
24- to 30-inch-diameter twig wreath base,
  like wild huckleberry or birch
Flat white spray paint
Gold spray paint
Clippers
Hot glue gun or low-temperature glue
  gun and glue sticks

## What You Do

1. Buy or make the twig wreath base. (See "Single-Wire Frame" on page 235 for instructions.) Lightly mist the wreath all over with white paint to give it a frosty winter look. Allow to dry.

2. Spray the leaves and pods with gold paint. Allow to dry.

3. Glue the leaves, then the various pods all around the wreath.

# The Holly and the Ivy

One of my favorite Christmas carols inspired this simple, fresh wreath. Add a spicy-oil scent to the greens for an aromatic version.

## What You Need

24 stems of fresh variegated ivy, each 8 to 10 inches long

8 cups of damp sphagnum moss or green sheet moss

36 stems of fresh holly, each 8 inches long

Bucket of water

14-inch-diameter flat wire wreath frame

Floral spool wire

3½ yards of red twisted paper ribbon

6 floral pins

Scented oil (Spice is nice.)

Clippers

Scissors

Wire cutters

## What You Do

1. Before working with fresh ivy, submerge it in a bucket of water overnight.

2. Place the damp moss around the wreath frame. Wrap with spool wire.

3. Divide the holly into 12 clusters of 3 stems each. Lay a cluster on the frame, with tips angling outward, and wrap with wire to secure. Wrap the remaining clusters until the frame is covered.

4. Remove the ivy from the water. Tuck the bottom of the ivy stems into the moss all the way around the wreath. They will continue to remain fresh as they absorb moisture from the moss.

5. Take 1½ yards of twisted paper ribbon and wind it loosely around the wreath. (Do not untwist the ribbon.) Pin the ribbon to the moss with floral pins.

6. Untwist the remaining 2 yards of ribbon and make a bow. (See "Making a Bow" on page 243.) Attach the bow to the wreath with spool wire.

7. Before hanging the wreath, sprinkle drops of scented oil directly onto the ivy in several out-of-the-way spots.

# Pink Pineapple

This composite of all-natural materials will surprise admirers with its offbeat color. It is one of the Christmas wreaths that continues to serve after the holiday and throughout the winter.

## What You Need

56 cuttings of fresh evergreens, with stems cut to 10 inches
6 fresh decorative pineapples (Note that these are decorative only, not edible.)
12 dried okra pods on stems
12 preserved magnolia leaves
6 or 7 dried stems of silver dollar plant
6 stems of pink pepperberries
14-inch-diameter wire wreath frame with clamps (The finished wreath is 30 inches in diameter.)
Bucket of water
6 lengths of floral wire, each about 10 inches long
12 to 24 floral picks
Clippers
Wire cutters
Hot glue gun and glue sticks

## What You Do

1. Make the wreath base by clamping bunches of evergreens onto the wire frame. (See "Wire Wreath Frame with Clamps" on page 236 for instructions.) Or start with a purchased wreath.

2. Trim the pineapple stems to 4 inches long and stand the pineapples in about 4 inches of water—just to cover the stems—for four hours to condition them.

3. Pierce through the lower quarter of each pineapple from side to side with the wire and bend the two wire ends down.

4. Position the six pineapples evenly around the wreath. Insert the two wire ends of each pineapple through the evergreens to the back of the wreath base and twist the ends together.

5. Cut the stems of the okra to 6 inches long and insert two between each pair of pineapples, pushing the stems into the thickness of the evergreens. (If your okra has tiny stems, use floral tape to tape the stems to sticks or to floral picks.)

6. Wrap the stems of the magnolia leaves onto floral picks and insert two by each pineapple.

7. Glue the stems of the silver dollar plant among the outer tips of the evergreens. Glue the stems of pepperberries among the inner pieces of the evergreens.

CHAPTER 6

# Wreaths in a Rainbow of colors

THE WREATHS IN THIS CHAPTER EMPHASIZE COLOR AND TEXTURE OVER SHAPE AND STYLE. ROMANTIC PINKS, BOLD REDS, BRILLIANT ORANGES, WARM YELLOWS, COOLING GREENS, SOOTHING BLUES, EARTHY BROWNS, SUBTLE GRAYS, AND PURE WHITES—EACH EVOKES A DIFFERENT MOOD. DECISIONS ARE EASY BECAUSE YOU NEED TO SEARCH FOR ONLY THREE OR FOUR MATERIALS IN THE COLOR RANGE. ADD EVEN ONE OTHER COLOR, AND YOU HAVE A TOTALLY DIFFERENT (ALSO WONDERFUL) APPEARANCE.

# white and Brown

*W*hite for brides. White for winter. Use everlastings for the truest color or go for a creamier version with roses and larkspur. Brown needn't be boring. Note the contrasts here between beige and chocolate.

## what You Need for the white wreath

Assortment of dried white everlastings (Here I used 8 strawflowers, 8 immortelle, 8 helipterum, and 6 stems of German statice.)

Clusters of dried Australian daisy, winged everlasting, and 'the Pearl' yarrow

14-inch-diameter vine wreath base

Matte white spray paint

1 ready-made or hand-tied bow of delicate white ribbon

2 white artificial birds (optional)

Clippers

Hot glue gun and glue sticks

## what You Do

1. Buy or make the vine wreath base. (See "Woven Vine" or "Wrapped Vine" on page 234 for instructions). Spray it with white paint and let it dry. Wire, glue, or tie the bow in place. (See "Making a Bow" on page 243.)

2. Cut the German statice into pieces with stems 4 to 6 inches long. Glue the statice all around the wreath. Then glue on clusters of the smaller flowers. If you try to use these stems individually, they won't show up well. Add the larger flowers, like the strawflowers and immortelle.

> ### ELLEN'S EXTRAS
> WHEN FLOWERS ARE NEWLY DRIED AND KEPT OUT OF DIRECT SUNLIGHT, THE STEMS SHOULD HAVE A GREENISH CAST, WHICH MAKES THEM LOOK FRESHER. WHEN YOU BUY DRIED FLOWERS, CHECK THE STEM COLOR AS WELL AS THE FLOWER COLOR TO ENSURE YOU'RE BUYING DRIED FLOWERS THAT ARE IN THEIR PRIME.

3. Glue the birds to the vine wreath near the ribbon, if desired.

## what You Need for the Brown wreath

Assortment of brown pods (Here I used 2 lotus, 7 okra, 3 teasel, and 6 sensitive fern pods.)

Assortment of brown leaves, collected in fall and pressed flat

4 stems of light brown leaves from a protea

20-inch-diameter vine wreath base (Here I used cat briar.)

Clippers

Hot glue gun and glue sticks

## What You Do

1. Buy or make the vine wreath base. (See "Woven Vine" or "Wrapped Vine" on page 234 for instructions.) Glue all of the materials directly to the base, starting with the largest first. Here I began with the lotus pods.

2. Next glue on the okra pods, with three or four on each side. As you can see, this wreath is not meant to be perfectly symmetrical, but the pods should all curve in the same direction.

3. Fill in with large leaf clusters and pods, like teasel and sensitive fern.

# Pink and Ruby Red

This delicate pink wreath is guaranteed to please any little (or big) girl with romantic inclinations. Merry Christmas or Happy Valentine's Day—this ruby red wreath suits both occasions as well as "velvet" winter weddings.

## What You Need for the Pink Wreath

16 stems of small dried cockscomb
30 to 40 stems of dried larkspur
14 dried strawflower heads

48-inch length of 20-gauge wire
Green floral tape
Floral spool wire
Clippers
Wire cutters
Hot glue gun and glue sticks
Tape measure or ruler

## What You Do

1. To make a triangular wreath frame, wrap the 20-gauge wire with green floral tape. Bend the wire 18 inches from the end to form the first side of the triangle. Measure another 12 inches and bend the wire to make the triangle. Allow the two wires to cross about 6 inches from the ends, as shown by point B in the illustration. Tape the wires under and over where they cross to secure the shape.

2. Break apart the cockscomb and larkspur into smaller pieces. Make bundles of two or three stems of one flower or a combination of both.

3. To add the flowers to the wreath frame, start at one end of the crossed wires, as shown by point A in the illustration. Tie a small cluster of flowers to the wreath frame with the spool wire. You will need to cut the stems as you go so they don't extend over the edges of the frame.

4. Tie the next cluster of flowers over the stems of the first cluster and continue until you reach point C. Then turn and go across to point D. Start again at point E, tying on the other flowers until you again reach point D.

5. Glue the strawflower heads in place. Glue on additional floral pieces at the end wherever the wreath might look a little sparse. You can use broken pieces or extra flowers cut from the larkspur stems to fill in.

## What You Need for the Red Wreath

38 heads of dried red cockscomb (The number will vary greatly depending on the size of the heads; here they were fairly small.)
3 dried red roses
14 small pieces of dried smooth sumac
12 dried red globe amaranths with leaves
10-inch-diameter straw wreath base
3 strands of red raffia
Clippers
Scissors
Hot glue gun and glue sticks

## What You Do

1. Glue the cockscomb all around the wreath, starting on the top and going down the sides. After gluing on the first piece, cover that stem with the next flower head to achieve a look of massed velvet. Here I haven't covered the sides completely. If a bit of straw shows, it won't detract from the look.

2. Take each strand of raffia, double it over, and make a small bow. Glue the three bows around the wreath.

3. Now continue to decorate by gluing on all the flowers: first the roses, one near each bow, then the sumac and the globe amaranths.

# Orange and Yellow

*W*hen fall approaches, Japanese lanterns and bittersweet are ready for picking. A mostly orange wreath announces the season. On this delicate yellow wreath, four varieties of dried flowers radiate the warmth of spring.

## What You Need for the Orange Wreath

15 dried Japanese lantern pods
25 dried orange strawflowers
5 stems of dried safflower
25 dried orange globe amaranths
17-inch-diameter bittersweet wreath base
Clippers
Hot glue gun and glue sticks

## What You Do

1. Make the bittersweet wreath base. (See "Woven Vine" or "Wrapped Vine" on page 234 for instructions.)

2. Separate the Japanese lanterns into five groups of three pods each. Space the groups as evenly as possible around the wreath base and glue them to the bittersweet.

3. Glue five strawflowers near each group of Japanese lantern pods. Glue a safflower stem between each group of pods and strawflowers. If the safflower clusters are large, cut off some individual flowers.

4. End with the smallest flowers, the globe amaranths. Glue these around the safflowers.

## What You Need for the Yellow Wreath

20 to 25 stems of fresh yellow statice
14 stems of dried golden drumstick
6 dried yellow strawflowers on wires
3 marigolds dried in silica gel and sprayed with a floral sealing spray
16-gauge wire
Floral spool wire
Clippers
Wire cutters
Hot glue gun and glue sticks

## WREATHMAKER'S WISDOM

*Wrap the statice while still fresh to minimize breakage. Allow the wreath to dry before adding other decorations. If your statice is already dry before you start making the wreath, mist it heavily with plain water and let the statice absorb the water for about 20 minutes. Most dried flowers abhor water but statice is an exception.*

*If you work with fresh material, remember that it will shrink when dried. Start with what seems like an overabundance to allow for the shrinkage.*

## What You Do

1. Make a 9-inch-diameter circle with the 16-gauge wire and twist the ends to secure. (See "Single-Wire Frame" on page 235 for instructions.)

2. Cut the stems of yellow statice to about 8 inches long. Each statice stem has many branches of flowers, so after cutting you will have more flower stems. Divide the statice cuttings into 20 piles.

3. Tie the spool wire onto the wire circle. Lay the first pile of statice on the circle with the flowers angling outward. Wrap securely with the spool wire. Add the next pile over the stems of the first and wrap it in place. Space the piles so you use ten piles to get halfway around the wire circle. Continue wrapping all the statice in this way until the circle is completely covered.

4. Cut the drumstick stems so they are 6 to 12 inches long. Glue seven drumsticks to each half of the wreath. Cut the strawflower wires to 3 to 4 inches and glue on the strawflowers. Then glue on the marigolds.

# Green and Blue

Think spring, think green. It is the perfect color to freshen up any dried wreath or arrangement. Combine shades of blue for the calming feeling of cool waters.

## What You Need for the Green Wreath

50 fresh galax leaves
30 fresh lemonleaf (salal) leaves
50 to 65 strands of fresh bear grass
12- to 14-inch-diameter vine wreath base
20- to 24-gauge floral spool wire
Clippers
Wire cutters
Hot glue gun and glue sticks

## What You Do

1. Buy or make the vine wreath base. (See "Woven Vine" or "Wrapped Vine" on page 234 for instructions.)

2. To form a galax leaf rosette, cut the stems of five leaves to ½ inch. Wrap the smallest leaf into a cone, with the point at the stem end. Secure with a dab of glue. Wrap the second leaf around the outside of the cone and glue in place. Add three other leaves to make one rosette. Repeat until you have made ten rosettes of five leaves each.

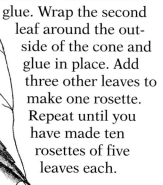

3. Glue the rosettes evenly around the wreath. Then glue the lemonleaf (salal) leaves between the rosettes. The leaves will curl as they dry.

4. Trim 3 inches off the bottom of the bear grass. Bundle the grass and tie it tightly with an 8-inch piece of spool wire, about 6 inches up from the bottom of the stems. Now tie the bundle to the top of the wreath with spool wire. Swing the bottom of the bundle over to the left and tie it to the wreath base. Since the stems shrink as they dry, the wrap must be very tight. Glue the spool wire for security. Hide the wire under a leaf or tie a strand of bear grass on top of it.

5. Allow the wreath to dry in a warm, dark, dry spot; or hang the wreath immediately and let it dry in place.

## What You Need for the Blue wreath

30 stems of dried blue statice
9 stems of dried globe thistle
2 heads of dried blue hydrangea
10-inch-diameter straw wreath base
30 to 40 floral pins
Clippers
Hot glue gun and glue sticks

## what You Do

1. Cut the stems of statice to 3 to 4 inches. Make a four- to five-piece cluster of stems and pin it to the straw wreath base. Make another cluster and pin it over the stems of the first. (See "Straw Wreath Base" on page 236 for instructions.) Cover the entire base with statice clusters, extending over the edges of the base by about 1½ inches.

2. Cut the stems of the globe thistle to 1 inch. Glue the globe thistle to the wreath in three groupings, as shown in the photo.

3. Cut the heads of the hydrangea into small clusters and individual florets. Glue eight clusters around the inside rim of the wreath. Scatter the other clusters and the florets around the wreath.

# Purple and Gray

The U-shape of this purple wreath allows you to hang it in
Unusual places, even Under another wreath. Tones of gray
make an ideal background for bright decoration,
or the gray can stand alone.

## What You Need for the Purple Wreath

60 stems of 2 shades of dried purple statice
30 to 40 stems of dried larkspur
20 to 30 stems of dried rat-tail statice
40 to 50 dried globe amaranths
16-gauge wire
Floral spool wire
Clippers
Wire cutters

## What You Do

1. To make a 20-inch-high finished wreath, cut the 16-gauge wire to 32 inches and form a U-shape. Make the uprights of uneven lengths. Bend over the tip of each end to make a little hook for hanging. Here the U-shape is 8 inches across the bottom and the uprights are 10 inches and 12 inches high.

2. Cut the flower stems as you go. The stems for the uprights should be about 10 inches long; the stems for the bottom of the wreath should be about 3 inches long. Tie the spool wire to the top of one upright. Make a cluster of six to eight assorted flower stems and wrap the stems to the frame with spool wire.

3. Take another cluster of flowers, lay it on top of the stems of the previous cluster, and wrap it to the frame with the spool wire. When you get to the bottom of the upright, turn the corner and wrap along the horizontal leg. Tie off and cut the spool wire. Start at the top of the other upright and attach the flowers in the same way.

## What You Need for the Gray Wreath

30 stems of dried 'Silver King' artemisia
30 stems of dried lamb's-ear
20 stems of dried poppy pods
20 stems of dried sage
20-gauge wire
Floral spool wire
Clippers
Wire cutters

## What You Do

1. To make a 26-inch-diameter finished wreath, make a 10-inch-diameter circle with the 20-gauge wire and twist the ends to secure. (See "Single-Wire Frame" on page 235 for instructions.)

2. Divide the floral materials into ten piles, each with the materials in this order from the bottom of the pile to the top: three stems of artemisia, three stems of lamb's-ear, two stems of poppy, and two stems of sage. Here the artemisia stems are about 9 inches long. Cut the lamb's-ear and poppy stems to 6 to 7 inches long. The sage is shortest, so it's on the top of the pile.

3. Tie the spool wire onto the wire circle. Now place one pile of material onto the ring and wrap tightly with the wire to hold securely. Place the second pile over the stems of the first and wrap securely again.

4. Continue adding the rest of the piles in this way. Be sure to space them so you don't run out of material before the wire is completely covered.

# wreaths
## in All Sizes

When designing a wreath, think of size as well as shape and color for a custom-made appearance. Giant wreaths adorn two-story spaces and should stay in proportion to the architectural scale. They need long branches, large leaves and flower heads, whole bunches of flowers, and extra-wide ribbons to decorate.

Miniature wreaths serve more delicate purposes and are usually viewed at close quarters. For place cards, tree ornaments, or gift decorations, tiny buds and berries fit the miniature theme. When you group a collection of miniatures together, you can equal the drama of a larger wreath.

# wreath Quilt

*I*f you're fascinated by quilts but don't have the skill or time to sew one, try this charming substitute. It won't keep you warm at night, but it is an outstanding decorative piece.

## what You Need

3 pieces of 14-inch-long, thin, pliable twig for each wreath (Here I used flowering crabapple.)

Assortment of dried flowers, like small roses and leaves, Australian daisy, and baby's-breath

Floral spool wire

18 × 27-inch mat board

¾ × 27-inch-long strip of decorative paper, like gift wrap or wallpaper

Two ¾ × 18-inch-long strips of decorative paper, like gift wrap or wallpaper

Picture frame without glass to fit the mat board

6 small ribbon bows (optional)

Clippers

Scissors or paper cutter

Hot glue gun and glue sticks

Glue for paper, like spray adhesive or rubber cement

Ruler

Pencil

## What You Do

1. Clasp three twigs at the bottom in your nonpreferred hand. With the other hand, bend the tips of two twigs down to form one side of a heart and grasp the tips. Bend the tip of the remaining twig down to form the other side of the heart. Wrap with spool wire to hold the shape. Make five more mini-wreaths in this way.

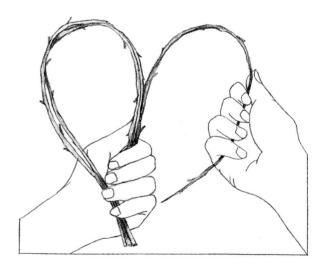

2. Plan the design of the quilt on the mat board. With the pencil and ruler, measure and mark six 9-inch squares, two across and three down.

# The Missing Link

*I*nterlock small vine wreaths the same way you made paper chains as a child. Adorn a window, a banister, or a Christmas tree. The chain will stay perfect for years; just change the decoration to fit the occasion.

## What You Need

Two 1-yard lengths of any fresh or pliable vine, about ¼ inch in diameter, for each wreath

2 bouquets of dried flowers, pods, grains, or grasses (Here I used cockscomb, hydrangea, plumed celosia, oriental nigella, and globe centaurea.)

A few sprigs of dried flowers (optional)

Floral spool wire

2 ribbon bows

Ribbon scrap (optional)

Clippers

Wire cutters

## What You Do

**1.** To make the first wreath, take two strands of vine and hold them together. Bend the tips down to form a 3-inch-diameter circle and hold in one hand. Still holding the strands in the same hand, wrap the rest of the vine around and around the circle and tuck in the ends. (See "Woven Vine" or "Wrapped Vine" on page 234 for instructions.) The finished wreath measures about 4 inches in diameter.

**2.** To make the second wreath and link it to the first, take two more yard-long strands of vine and put the ends through the first wreath. Next form a 3-inch-diameter circle and wrap the

vine as you did in Step 1. As you work, the first wreath may get in your way. To minimize this, keep spinning the first wreath away from the place you are working, letting it hang free.

**3.** Repeat Step 2 to make and join as many wreaths as you desire. The chain here has 26 wreaths linked together. It is made without any wire, but if you feel insecure, cut off small pieces of the spool wire and use them to hold up any weak wreaths. There is a tendency to let the wreaths get larger and larger as you work down the chain. Be wary of this possibility and compare your work against the first wreath every once in a while.

**4.** When your wreath chain is complete, wrap each floral bouquet with the spool wire. Leave enough wire to tie the bouquet to the chain; cut off any extra wire. Here I've concentrated the decoration at the two draping points, wiring on two bows and two bouquets of dried flowers. I made the center decoration from a ribbon scrap and a few flower sprigs. However, you can decorate your wreath chain any way you want. Instead of using the bouquets, you could glue tiny flowers on each wreath or tuck small bits of boxwood between the wrapped vines of each wreath.

# Spicy Tree Ornaments and Mini-Wreaths for Packages

For a warm and welcoming effect, trim a tree with dried peppers for color and mini-wreaths of spice beads for fragrance. To individualize a gift, attach a small floral wreath to the bow.

## What You Need for the Ornaments

1 cup of ground cinnamon or combination of ground cinnamon, cloves, ginger, nutmeg, and allspice in any proportion
1 cup of thick applesauce
2 tablespoons of ground orrisroot (order from your local pharmacy or herb shop)
Mixing spoon
Bowl and plate
1 box of round wooden toothpicks
1 sheet of wax paper
20-gauge copper or gold wire
Assortment of decorative beads
Pencil
Clippers
Wire cutters

## What You Do

1. With a mixing spoon, mix the spices, applesauce, and orrisroot in a bowl until thoroughly combined. As with other doughs, you may need to adjust the consistency. If too crumbly, add another tablespoon or so of applesauce. If too wet, add a little more ground spice.

2. Make balls the size of a large marble by rolling pieces of dough between your palms. Make other sizes as desired.

3. Insert a toothpick through the center of each ball and wiggle it slightly to enlarge the hole. Leave the toothpick in each ball. The dough shrinks as it dries, and you want to keep the hole open for stringing. Set the balls aside to dry on a plate covered with wax paper. It will take between 24 and 48 hours for them to dry completely.

4. When the balls are dry, cut 18 inches of wire for each ornament. String several spice balls, interspersing them with the decorative beads. The spice balls must be handled gently because they can break apart.

5. When you are pleased with the results, gently twist the two ends of the wire together at the top to hold the wreath form together, or tie the wire into a small bow. You can spiral the wire ends by wrapping them around the pencil. Then remove the pencil. If you want extra spirals, make them out of additional pieces of wire and wrap them around the wreath.

## What You Need
## for 1 Mini-Wreath

Assortment of small dried flowers
Miniature vine wreath base
Clippers
Hot glue gun and glue sticks

## What You Do

1. Buy or make the vine wreath base. (See "Woven Vine" or "Wrapped Vine" on page 234 for instructions.)

2. Glue the assortment of dried flowers all around the wreath.

3. Attach the wreath to a package by tying it to the ends of the package ribbon.

# For the Birds: A Maxi-Wreath

*F*un to make and fun to observe afterward, this bird feeder wreath will decorate any large, outdoor space. To get the most pleasure from this wreath, hang it where you can see the avian action from indoors.

## What You Need

Fresh pine or other evergreen branches,
   each 12 to 16 inches long
6 dried sunflower heads with seeds
12 or more dried ears of corn (Here I
   used strawberry corn.)
42-inch-diameter extruded foam wreath
   base
10 yards of ribbon, suitable for outdoors
22-gauge floral spool wire
2 or more bags of suet wrapped in netting
   (Here I used what I saved from onion
   sacking for the netting.)
5 or more fresh rinds of grapefruit halves
Birdseed or peanut butter
2 bags of fresh cranberries, 12 ounces each
Clippers
Scissors
Wire cutters

## What You Do

1. Identify the top of the wreath by finding
   the wreath hanger on the back of the
   wreath base. As you decorate, keep the
   hanger location in mind so you get no
   unpleasant surprises at the end.

2. Cover the wreath base with the evergreen branches, using the wrapping
   method described in "Single-Wire
   Frame" on page 235.

3. Cut the ribbon into two 5-yard lengths
   and make two bows. (See "Making a
   Bow" on page 243 for instructions.)
   Leave the tails 2 to 3 feet long.

4. Nestle the loops of the two bows
   together and wrap with spool wire.
   You will have one big bow with four
   tails. Wire the bow to the wreath,
   draping the tails down each side.

5. Poke two small holes in the sides of
   each sunflower with the scissor point
   and run a 15-inch length of spool wire
   through the holes. Place the sunflower
   on the evergreen wreath base. Wrap the
   wires around the back of the wreath
   and twist to secure.

6. Twist pieces of spool wire around the
   stems of corn and then around the
   evergreen branches to secure the corn
   to the branches. Then wire the bags of
   suet around the back of the foam
   wreath base, not just around the
   greens, because they are heavy.

7. Make wire handles for the grapefruit
   halves, so they look like baskets, and
   hang them on evergreen branches.
   After the wreath is hung, fill them with
   birdseed or peanut butter.

8. String the cranberries on 3- to 4-yard
   lengths of spool wire. This can be done
   one to two weeks ahead of decorating
   the wreath if you keep the strands in
   the refrigerator until you are ready to
   use them. Two bags of cranberries will
   make about four strands, each 2 to 3
   yards long. Simply pierce the cranberry
   with the wire and move it along like a
   bead. Leave 6 to 8 inches of wire at
   each end to wrap the strands in place
   around the wreath.

9. Swag the strands along the front of
   the wreath, two on each side. Take
   extra small pieces of wire and secure
   the strands in several places so they
   will drape where you want them to
   and not just plop down. You can
   also secure the tails of the ribbon
   with small pieces of wire to keep it
   draped properly.

# The Friendly Giant

When you have a cathedral wall to decorate, a tall fireplace, a church, or an office building—don't be shy. Massive space requires massive flowers. Use flowers in bunches rather than individually.

## What You Need

Assortment of 50 to 65 bunches of dried flowers
3-foot-diameter sturdy vine wreath base
Floral spool wire
Clippers
Wire cutters

## What You Do

1. Buy or make a sturdy vine wreath base. (See "Woven Vine" or "Wrapped Vine" on page 234 for instructions.) Here the wreath is grapevine, but very little of it shows. It serves mainly as a structure to hold the dried flowers.

2. It's best to construct this wreath while it's hanging. Find a nail or hook somewhere in a work area; later transport it to where it will be displayed.

3. Tie each bunch of flowers to the wreath base with a 10- to 12-inch-long piece of spool wire. This is a change from the standard technique of wrapping with a continuous spool. Tying each bunch on separately allows you to change angles and also provides extra security. Tie on the bunches starting at the top of the wreath base and continuing clockwise, changing angles as you go. Snip off the excess wire.

# where Morning glories climb

$\mathcal{M}$ake a wreath to function as a natural trellis for your vines. The photo below shows the wreath soon after the morning glories started their climb. In the photo on the right, the wreath is almost completely hidden by the blooming vines.

## what You Need

Vine or twig wreath base, 48 or more inches in diameter
Exterior wall near a bed of vine seeds
Spool of string
Clippers
Scissors

## what You Do

1. Buy or make a vine or twig wreath base. (See "Woven Vine" or "Wrapped Vine" on page 234 for instructions.) This one is a birch twig wreath made on a 14-inch-diameter wire wreath frame with clamps. The birch branches are about 17 inches long. (See "Wire Wreath Frame with Clamps" on page 236 for instructions.)

2. Hang the wreath about 24 inches off the ground above the bed where you planted the vine seeds. As the vines start to shoot upward, help them to find the wreath by tying them to the wreath with string. Cut off the string after the tendrils are secured to the wreath.

### ELLEN'S EXTRAS

IN WINTER, LEAVE THE WREATH IN PLACE AND DECORATE IT WITH WINTER GREENS AND A BOW FOR A TOTALLY DIFFERENT FEEL. IF YOU HAVE A TWIG WREATH, YOU CAN SLIP SOME GREENS IN EACH CLAMP WHILE THE WREATH IS STILL HANGING. IF YOU HAVE A VINE WREATH, SLIP THE GREENS SECURELY UNDER THE WRAPPING WIRES.

# Big, Bold, and Beautiful

*M*any occasions and locations demand oversized wreaths. In this great room with a cathedral ceiling, a puny wreath would be swallowed up. Be generous with your materials, and you will be rewarded.

## What You Need

98 stems of fresh lemonleaf (salal)
12 stems of dried burgundy plumed celosia
12 locust pods
14-inch-diameter wire wreath frame with clamps (The finished wreath is 42 inches in diameter.)
5 yards of wire-edged ribbon, 3 to 4 inches wide (Here I used 3 yards of one kind and 2 of another.)
20 inches of 24-gauge wire
Gold spray paint
Clippers
Wire cutters
Scissors
Hot glue gun and glue sticks

## What You Do

1. Cut the lemonleaf (salal) stems to 12 to 14 inches long. Save the clippings.

2. Take seven stems of lemonleaf (salal), place them in a wreath clamp, and clamp tightly. Add seven more stems in the next clamp, overlapping and hiding the stems of the first. Continue filling all the clamps in this way.

3. Turn the wreath over. In the back of each clamp, stuff enough stem trimmings to wedge the branches in tightly. They will shrink when dry, so be sure that each clamp is as tight as possible. Hang or lay the wreath flat for about two weeks until the leaves dry.

4. Make two large bows and wire them together so they look like one. (See "Making a Bow" on page 243.) Wire this construction to one side of the wreath.

5. Spray the locust pods with gold paint and let dry. Glue them around the wreath. Tuck the celosia stems in the clamps where possible or glue them around the wreath.

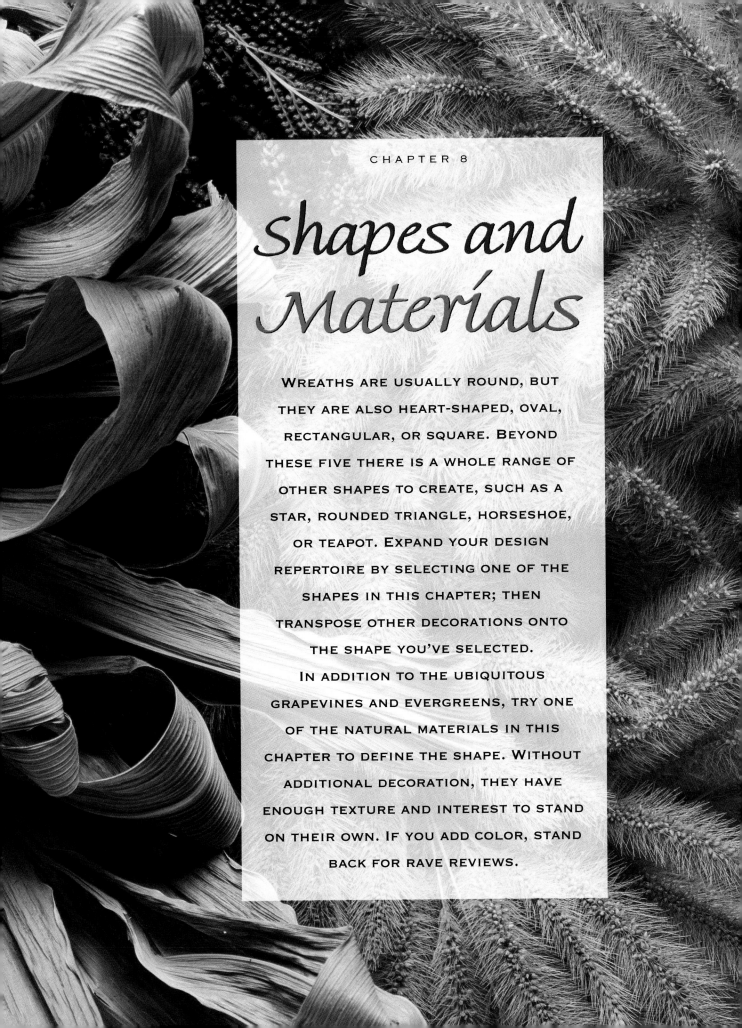

# shapes and Materials

WREATHS ARE USUALLY ROUND, BUT THEY ARE ALSO HEART-SHAPED, OVAL, RECTANGULAR, OR SQUARE. BEYOND THESE FIVE THERE IS A WHOLE RANGE OF OTHER SHAPES TO CREATE, SUCH AS A STAR, ROUNDED TRIANGLE, HORSESHOE, OR TEAPOT. EXPAND YOUR DESIGN REPERTOIRE BY SELECTING ONE OF THE SHAPES IN THIS CHAPTER; THEN TRANSPOSE OTHER DECORATIONS ONTO THE SHAPE YOU'VE SELECTED.

IN ADDITION TO THE UBIQUITOUS GRAPEVINES AND EVERGREENS, TRY ONE OF THE NATURAL MATERIALS IN THIS CHAPTER TO DEFINE THE SHAPE. WITHOUT ADDITIONAL DECORATION, THEY HAVE ENOUGH TEXTURE AND INTEREST TO STAND ON THEIR OWN. IF YOU ADD COLOR, STAND BACK FOR RAVE REVIEWS.

# Bark House and Woodland Initial

Tree bark is free and easily gathered and glued. Keep the pieces small if you want a round shape and long if you want an edifice. Initials, such as *P, O,* and *C,* lend themselves naturally to round wreaths. Others, like the *S* in the photo, take a stretch of imagination. But if you can hang it, why not make it?

## What You Need for the House

10 to 14 strips of bark (See "Wreath-maker's Wisdom" on this page.)
Bucket of hot water
Clippers
Hot glue gun and glue sticks

## What You Do

1. Soak the bark in a bucket of very hot water for about an hour to remove dirt and lurking insects. Spread it out and allow to dry.

2. Sort through the pieces of bark, saving the longest strips for the roof. Form the sides and bottom of the house into a square or rectangular shape. Map out the placement before you actually glue, trying pieces like a jigsaw puzzle until you have the best effect. For a more natural look, break or tear pieces when you need shorter pieces and use the clippers only as a last resort.

### WREATHMAKER'S WISDOM

Collect fallen bark at the base of trees or strip it from cut firewood—one of my favorite sources for birch bark. I once startled my new daughter-in-law by stripping every log she was getting ready to throw into their fireplace. Look for trees that shed naturally, such as shagbark and sycamore. Each texture will produce a totally different wreath base.

3. Glue the sides and bottom together in one layer, then add another layer for extra dimension. If you need longer pieces, just glue two pieces together.

4. Glue the roofline on last. Exert pressure on the joint for 30 to 45 seconds, until the glue sets.

# What You Need for the Initial

Assortment of dried fungi and bracken
(See "Ellen's Extras" on this page.)
Green sheet moss
Green-coated chicken wire
Floral spool wire
Clippers
Wire cutters
Hot glue gun and glue sticks

# What You Do

1. Decide on the finished size of your initial; here it is 18 inches tall. Cut the chicken wire in a strip 8 to 10 inches wide and as long as you need. For certain initials, like *K, R,* and *T,* cut two or more strips in the appropriate lengths.

2. Fold the chicken wire in thirds the long way. Take this strip and practice making the initial until you are satisfied with the shape.

3. Open the folds of the chicken wire and stuff the length with the sheet moss, green side down. Refold the chicken wire. You must make sure it will stay closed either by

## ELLEN'S EXTRAS

YOU CAN PURCHASE BRACKEN AND FUNGI ALREADY DRIED. SOME COME WITH PICKS ALREADY GLUED IN; THESE ARE VERY HELPFUL FOR WREATHMAKING. IF YOU COLLECT YOUR OWN MATERIALS ON YOUR PROPERTY, LOOK FOR MATERIALS ONLY ON FALLEN LIMBS OR DEAD TREES. SINCE FRESH WOODLAND MATERIALS CAN HARBOR TINY INSECTS, SWISH THEM IN SOAPY WATER AND LET THEM AIR-DRY. THEN DEHYDRATE THE MATERIALS IN THE OVEN (ON A COOKIE SHEET COVERED WITH WAX PAPER) FOR TWO HOURS AT 150°F.

weaving the ends of the cut chicken wire together, or by cutting some lengths of spool wire and lacing up the back.

4. You should now have a stuffed tube that is green on one side. Rebend it into the shape of the initial. If you are using more than one tube, attach the tubes with the spool wire.

5. Glue the fungi and bracken to the initial. Here I have emulated the way these materials grow by gluing the shelf bracken horizontally in clusters of layers and gluing the gray bracken flat on the form.

# crossed-Grapevine wreaths

Simple grapevine wreaths nestled one inside the other create an unusual look. Decorate like a kissing ball for Christmas or suspend suet and seed treats from it for the birds. Add a third wreath for a globe effect.

## what You Need

4 strands of grapevine, each 6 to 8 feet long
Floral spool wire
Clippers
Wire cutters
Tape measure or ruler

## what You Do

1. Make the first grapevine wreath by clasping the end of one strand of vine with one hand. With your other hand, bring the strand around to form a 12½-inch-diameter circle. (See page 120 for an illustration of this technique.) Grasp the circle at the top and keep winding. Add a second strand of vine in the same way.

2. Still clutching the vines, tie them together with the spool wire where you have been holding them. Wind the spool wire around the wreath to make all the strands behave. The circle should be neat. Tie off the wire and cut.

3. Repeat Steps 1 and 2 to make a 13-inch-diameter wreath in the same way; the inside mea-

surement of this wreath should be ½ inch larger than the outside measurement of the first wreath you made. When you are finished and ready to cut off the spool wire, leave an extra 12 inches of wire to bind the two wreaths together at the top and to hang the project. You can tie the wreaths together at the bottom with a little piece of wire or leave them untied for a mobile effect.

# Bittersweet Oval

$\mathcal{M}$ake this wreath in early fall with freshly cut bittersweet. You may want to add other seasonal materials like grains or Japanese lanterns to dress up the background.

## What You Need

10 to 12 freshly cut strands of full-berried bittersweet
Clippers

## What You Do

1. Using the bittersweet, make a vine wreath. (See "Woven Vine" or "Wrapped Vine" on page 234 for instructions.) Loop the first strand into an oval shape rather than a circle.

2. As you weave each strand into the wreath, continue to form the oval shape. Vines with this wild shape often seem to have a mind of their own and some strands will be less cooperative than others. But even the unruly ones add a certain charm to the finished wreath.

# Horseshoe Wreath of Pods and Cones

*A*ssemble diverse pods and cones to make this long-lasting design. Hang the horseshoe up, down, or sideways—depending on your version of tradition.

## what You Need

Assortment of cones and pods of different shapes and sizes (You can use pine, spruce, sweet gum, okra, lotus, hemlock, or whatever you have available.)

14-inch-diameter wire box frame

Bucket of warm water

Gold spray paint (optional)

Clippers

Heavy-duty wire cutters

Hot glue gun and glue sticks

## what You Do

1. To make a horseshoe from the wire box frame, use the wire cutters and some muscle to cut out one section of the wire frame; discard that section. Push the two sides of the frame together slightly to improve the shape.

2. Cones with open "petals," like pine, will close up if soaked in warm water for about 30 minutes. Soak these cones to make them easier to insert in the frame. Decide on a pattern. Start by inserting the long, thin pods and cones under the two center wires of the frame, as shown in the illustration on page 10. Continue around the horse-

shoe until the frame is full. Set it aside for several days until the cones dry and reopen.

3. Glue smaller cones around the horseshoe on top of the other cones, hiding the wires of the frame. To make a focal point, glue or wire on additional cones. Here I've used purchased lotus pods with wire stems attached. Cut the stems as short as necessary to wrap around the frame. Spray the wreath with gold paint, if desired.

# Kiwi Vine Abstract

Since kiwi vine loops and swirls as it grows, go with the flow. Let the vines dictate the outcome of your wreath.

## What You Need

12 to 18 strands of fresh-cut kiwi vine
(Here they are 1½ to 3 feet long.)
Tub of hot water
Floral spool wire
Clippers
Wire cutters

## What You Do

1. If your vine is not freshly cut, immerse it in a deep tub of hot water for 24 hours to make it pliable.

### ELLEN'S EXTRAS

IF YOU DON'T GROW KIWI VINE, MANY FLORISTS SELL IT BY THE PIECE, OR THEY CAN ORDER IT FOR YOU. YOU CAN SUBSTITUTE CONTORTED HAZEL OR CORKSCREW WILLOW AND FOLLOW THE SAME DIRECTIONS. EACH OF THESE MATERIALS WILL MAKE AN ABSTRACT WREATH, BUT THE FINISHED PRODUCT WILL LOOK COMPLETELY DIFFERENT FROM THE WREATH SHOWN HERE.

2. Start with your two longest strands. Wrap them together end to end with the spool wire. Cut the wire off the spool and tie it. Bring the opposite ends of the vine around to meet and intertwine with each other. This first wrap will determine the approximate size of the wreath. Don't try to make a wreath under 15 inches in diameter, or you'll get too tangled amid the vines.

3. Add other strands of vine one at a time. You will be able to interweave most of the vines among the others that are already done without any added wire. Where you need to for extra security, cut 6-inch lengths of spool wire and tie strands of the wreath together. The wreath shown in the photo has three such ties.

# Nuts To You

Some of these nuts came from my trees, some came from the supermarket, and some came from a friend of a friend of a friend—Texas by way of Santa Fe to Orwigsburg, Pennsylvania.

## What You Need

Assortment of nuts, whole or shelled
Corrugated cardboard
1 floral pin
Glossy polyurethane or shellac spray
Utility knife
Hot glue gun and glue sticks
Ruler
Pencil

## What You Do

1. Place the nuts on a cookie sheet and bake in a 200°F oven for two hours to kill any insects. Hot-glue any acorn caps that come loose before constructing the wreath.

2. Measure and mark a rectangle on the cardboard. Here the size is 11 × 14 inches. Cut out the rectangle with the utility knife. Cut an opening in the center of the rectangle, either a smaller rectangle or, as here, an oval.

3. Push the floral pin through the top of the cardboard base and bend it back to make the hanger. (See "How to Hang a Wreath" on page 240 for instructions.)

4. Decide on a pattern for the nuts and lay them out so that you know you have enough for your needs. My designs for a project are always partly based on which materials are scarce versus which I have in abundance. Here I glued a border of chestnuts around the outer edge, then a border of a mystery nut around the inner edge. Extend the nuts slightly over the edge to hide the cardboard.

5. Fill in the face of the wreath, then build it up by gluing nuts on top of others. Spray with the polyurethane following the manufacturer's directions.

# Briar Arch and Sorghum Swirl

This cat briar arch is particularly wonderful because the thorns add texture, and the color stays green for a long time. Sorghum is grown for feed or syrup. But when used in a wreath, the texture of the kernels is very attractive.

## What You Need for the Arch

20 strands of cat briar or other vine, each 4 to 8 feet long
Leather gloves to work with thorny vines
22- or 24-gauge spool wire (optional)
Clippers
Wire cutters (optional)

## What You Do

1. Wearing the leather gloves, make the horizontal base of the arch first. Take one strand of vine and lay out enough for the base, about 24 inches. Bend the vine just past the 24-inch mark and bring it back along itself, weaving it under and over and back and forth until you judge the base to be thick enough. I made this wreath with no wire—the briar strands support each other. If you have trouble holding your vine together, cut 4-inch lengths of wire and wrap the ends of the strands to secure.

2. To make the arch, take a strand of vine and insert one end through one end of the base. Bend this strand to form a graceful arch, bringing the other end of the vine down and inserting it through the other end of the base. Cut the excess vine here, or bend it back upon itself and weave it around the arch.

3. Continue to add strands of vine to the arch, weaving each new one around the other strands of arch until you reach the desired thickness.

4. Cut nine straight 15-inch-long pieces of vine for the trellis fan. Slip one piece in the center of the wreath, with one end inserted between the base strands and

the other end inserted between the strands at the top of the arch. Place four other pieces on each side of the center vine, spacing them as evenly as possible and always starting from the bottom center. Trim the ends where they stick out above the wreath.

## What You Need for the Swirl

55 stalks of dried sorghum with leaves
10-inch-diameter wire wreath frame with clamps
Clippers
Hot glue gun and glue sticks

## What You Do

1. Cut the tops of the stalks to about 18 inches long. Set aside the leaves and bottoms of the stalks.

2. Put four stalks of sorghum in the first wreath clamp and close tightly. (See "Wire Wreath Frame with Clamps" on page 236 for instructions.).

3. Go around the frame, putting four stalks in each clamp, overlapping the previous stems. In the last clamp, work the stems under the heads of the first group.

4. You will have 15 stalks left. Check your wreath. If any of the clamps show, stick in a stalk or glue an extra leaf over the clamp to hide it.

# corn-Leaves Oval

*O*rdinary corn leaves dry with extraordinary flair. The simple oval shape of this wreath repeats the bend of each leaf.

## what You Need

90 fresh corn leaves
14-inch-diameter straw wreath base
60 floral pins
Clippers
Hot glue gun and glue sticks

## what You Do

1. Wash the leaves to clean them of dust, dirt, and insects. Let dry briefly. You'll be working with the leaves while they're still fresh. They will dry completely after they are pinned in place. Save a few leaves for filling in bare or uneven spots after the wreath has dried.

2. Fold over a leaf to make a loop. Fold over three more leaves in the same way and pin the cluster to the wreath base. Continue looping leaves and pinning them on in clusters of three or four, always overlapping the stems of the previous leaves. Cut the stems as necessary if the loops are too long for the wreath size you desire. Alter the angles of the clusters as you go, pinning one cluster angling out over the edge, another in the middle of the wreath base, and another angling toward the center.

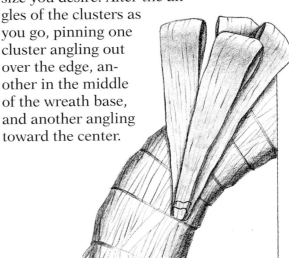

# Rounded Magnolia Triangle

The glossy leaves of the southern magnolia tree display their shape and texture in a bold and artful way without any other embellishment.

## What You Need

45 to 50 preserved magnolia leaves
6 dried magnolia cones
12-inch-diameter straw wreath base
100 floral pins
Clippers

## WREATHMAKER'S WISDOM

*Preserved magnolia leaves, like preserved eucalyptus and juniper, have been dyed and will sometimes exude a glycerine "sweat" if they are exposed to too much humidity. This may stain paint, so don't put this wreath or other dyed, preserved material on a light-colored door where it may get wet.*

*If some leaves are too large for your needs or are ragged around the edges, trim them with the clippers. Try to keep to the natural shape, and they will look neat and pretty without cracking or crumbling in the process.*

## What You Do

1. Referring to the illustrations on page 6, pin the leaves, dull side up, to the wreath base, using 2 pins on each leaf and pointing the tips of the leaves outward. Go three-quarters of the way around the wreath and use 13 leaves.

2. Turn the wreath over to the "good" side. The leaves you have already pinned form a halo around the outside of the wreath. Now work on the face of the wreath by pinning the leaves in a circle around the wreath, overlapping as you go to hide the previous pin. Use one pin for each leaf.

3. Pin three magnolia cones along the bottom of the wreath, and three cones evenly spaced around the circle. Pin the stem of each cone tightly to the wreath, hiding the pin under a leaf.

# Cotton Boll Oval and Wisteria Diamond

*It*'s almost impossible to keep from touching the softness of this cotton boll wreath. Thick, gnarled wisteria vines are soft enough to cut yet rigid enough to nail and hold their shape.

## What You Need for the Oval

42 cotton bolls (available from flower-craft suppliers or florists)
1 sheet of newspaper
Corrugated cardboard from a carton, at least 12 × 15 inches
1 piece of floral wire or 1 floral pin
4 strands of natural raffia
Scissors
Utility knife
Hot glue gun and glue sticks
Ruler or tape measure
Pencil

## What You Do

1. Using the ruler, pencil, and scissors, draw and cut out one 11 × 14-inch rectangle from the newspaper. To make an oval pattern, fold the paper rectangle in half and round out the corners. By folding the paper in half you ensure even sides when you open it. Measure and mark 2½ inches from each edge toward the center and cut out this center hole in an oval shape.

2. To make the cardboard wreath base, trace the oval pattern onto the cardboard and cut it out with the scissors.

3. Make a wreath hanger with either the wire or the floral pin. (See "How to Hang a Wreath" on page 240 for instructions.)

4. If you don't grow your own cotton, purchase bolls by the bag. Many of the bolls are overflowing with cotton so you can hardly see the pod. The cotton also may need cleaning because little bits of dried leaves or seeds are often stuck to the fibers. Take each pod and carefully pull out the excess cotton from each section, thereby exposing the attractive pod segments and cleaning the fibers.

5. Take six pods and remove all the cotton fibers. Set aside. Cut off all the stems of the remaining pods.

6. Glue the pods with the cotton to the cardboard wreath base; two will fit across the 2½-inch width of the base. Fill in all the spaces so the cardboard edges don't show.

7. Double over the raffia strands and make a simple bow. Trim the ends short and glue the bow to the top of the wreath.

8. Take the six reserved pods without fibers and glue them around the wreath for added depth.

## what You Need for the Diamond

Wisteria or other vine as thick as your thumb: four 15-inch-long pieces and one 8-inch-long piece
Wisteria or other vine as thick as your little finger: two 13-inch-long pieces
4 finishing nails
Hammer
Pruning saw
Clippers
Hot glue gun and glue sticks
Tape measure or ruler

## what You Do

1. Referring to the photo on the opposite page, arrange the four 15-inch-long pieces of vine into a square so that the pieces intersect 3½ inches from the ends. Bang one finishing nail into each intersection. The wreath will not be perfectly even because of the interesting twists of the vines. You may have to place the first nail slightly off the 3½-inch mark. If so, simply change the other three intersections accordingly.

2. Rotate the square so it looks like a diamond with one of the corners pointing toward you. Glue the 13-inch pieces in an X across the middle of the diamond.

3. Saw or cut five ½-inch-thick rounds of vine from the 8-inch piece of vine. Glue one in the center and four over the finishing nails, as shown in the photo.

# shells and sponges

These shells represent a trip I made to Florida 12 years ago.
They languished in a box until I began this wreath. Natural
sponges in a star shape also depict the shore look.

## what You Need
## for the Shell Wreath

Assortment of shells
Several handfuls of fresh or dried
    Spanish moss
19-inch-square of corrugated cardboard

17-inch-diameter mixing bowl
    or plate
3-inch-diameter glass or mug
1 floral pin
Acrylic spray or shellac (optional)
Scissors or utility knife
Hot glue gun and glue sticks
Pencil

## What You Do

1. To make the wreath base, use the pencil to trace a circle about 17 inches in diameter onto the cardboard. A large mixing bowl or dinner plate makes a good template for this. Now draw a five-pointed star, coming to the edges of the circle. Since I wanted this wreath to resemble a starfish rather than a traditional star, each point is curved rather than straight. Cut out the star with a scissors or utility knife.

2. In the center of the star, trace another circle about 3 inches in diameter using a glass or mug as the template. Cut out this smaller circle.

3. Make a hanger using the floral pin. (See "How to Hang a Wreath" on page 240 for instructions.)

4. Glue all the shells to the cardboard wreath base with hot glue, building up in layers. Lay out a bottom layer first. The pattern will depend on the size and shape of the shells you have gathered. Here I glued on a circle of oyster shells in the middle, overlapping them as I went. Then I glued on the small conch shells at the tips, extending over the cardboard a bit to hide the wreath base. As you fit the shells, try to emphasize the starfish shape and cover most of the cardboard.

5. Glue on the Spanish moss last, hiding the exposed cardboard and filling in any gaps between the shells. Spray with shiny acrylic for a wet look, if desired.

## What You Need for the Sponge Wreath

2 natural sponges, each about the size of an eggplant (Or you can use man-made sponges that look like natural ones.)
Several handfuls of fresh or dried Spanish moss
19-inch-square of corrugated cardboard
17-inch-diameter mixing bowl or plate
3-inch-diameter glass or mug
1 floral pin
Acrylic spray or shellac (optional)
Scissors or utility knife
Hot glue gun and glue sticks
Pencil

## What You Do

1. Follow Steps 1 through 3 for the "Shell Wreath" on the left. Then wet the sponges and tear them into small pieces. Glue them onto the wreath base, being sure to cover all of the cardboard. Let the sponges dry in place before proceeding.

2. Drape and glue the Spanish moss on top of the sponge for a rather dramatic finishing touch.

### ELLEN'S EXTRAS

IF YOU NEED SHELLS TO ROUND OUT A COLLECTION, PLAN A DINNER OF MUSSELS MARINARA OR CLAM STEW AND GO TO YOUR LOCAL FISH MARKET. IF ALL ELSE FAILS, CHECK OUT THE LOCAL CRAFT STORES. MOST SELL PACKAGES OF BEAUTIFUL SHELLS. RUN YOUR SHELLS THROUGH THE DISHWASHER IN THE UTENSIL HOLDER TO CLEAN BEFORE USE.

# Sensitive Fern Square and Catalpa Pod Triangle

This square wreath frames any special picture, diploma, or certificate. The chocolate brown of the sensitive fern boldly outlines the material within. Catalpa, locust, or other long, thin tree pods are free for the gathering. Use them for a rustic look.

# What You Need for the Square

230 stems of sensitive fern
16-gauge floral spool wire
22- or 26-gauge floral spool wire
Polyurethane spray (optional)
Clippers
Wire cutters
Ruler or tape measure

## What You Do

1. Cut 50 inches of 16-gauge spool wire with the wire cutters. Make a square wreath base that is 10 inches on each side. Use the extra 10 inches of wire for wrapping around the square to hold it together securely.

2. Cut the sensitive fern to 9 inches long. Tie the 22-gauge spool wire onto the frame at one corner. Take a bundle of seven fern stems and angle them outward slightly, away from the wreath base. Wrap them tightly to the base with the spool wire. Take another bundle of seven fern stems. Lay them over the stems of the first bundle and wrap in place. Continue wrapping six more bundles along the side. As you get nearer the opposite corner, cut the stems shorter, so they won't peek out from the bottom of the wreath. Turn the corner and keep bunching and wrapping back to the starting point.

3. Tie off and cut the spool wire. Tuck in any extra stems wherever the wreath appears uneven. Spray it with polyurethane, if desired. The finished square is 20 inches tall.

# What You Need for the Triangle

150 catalpa pods
22- or 26-gauge floral spool wire
16-gauge floral spool wire
Polyurethane spray (optional)
Clippers
Wire cutters
Ruler or tape measure

## What You Do

1. Cut 46 inches of 16-gauge wire with the wire cutters. Make a triangular wreath base with two 12-inch-long sides and one 18-inch-long side. Use the extra wire to secure the ends together.

2. Leave the catalpa pods whole—just trim off the stems with the clippers. Tie the 22-gauge spool wire to the base at one corner.

3. Make bundles of three to four pods and wrap them tightly to the base with the wire. Wrap the wire very tightly so the pods don't fall out. Continue wrapping bundles to the base until you return to the starting point.

4. Tie off and cut the spool wire. Tuck in any extra pods wherever the wreath appears uneven. Spray with polyurethane to deepen the color and protect the pods if the wreath will be exposed to the elements.

# Six Vine Wreaths in Unusual Shapes

Round or oval wreaths form the bases for all six of these designs. Add other small vine pieces to give each its distinctive shape. Enlarge or reduce the base size or add extra dried flowers to customize your work.

## What You Need for Each Wreath

Fresh, pliable strands of vine, like grape, honeysuckle, or bittersweet
Dried flowers and leaves (Here I've mostly used air-dried roses.)
Floral spool wire
Green sheet moss
Clippers
Wire cutters
Hot glue gun and glue sticks

## What You Do for the Basket

1. In addition to the wreath materials listed above, you will need one 12-inch-long twig, the thickness of your finger, and 3 yards of ribbon for a bow.

2. Using the strands of pliable vine, make a 12-inch-diameter round wreath base. (See "Woven Vine" or "Wrapped Vine" on page 234 for instructions.)

3. Insert the 12-inch-long twig horizontally across the middle of the wreath; you now have a basket with a handle.

4. Turn the basket over to the "wrong" side and run hot glue just around the bottom portion of the basket. Press on a whole piece of sheet moss, green side down, to the back bottom portion.

5. Turn the basket right side up and trim any excess moss. Wire a small bunch of dried flowers and a bow to the wreath at the handle.

## What You Do for the Teapot

1. Using the strands of vine, make a 12 × 15-inch oval wreath base. (See "Woven Vine" or "Wrapped Vine" on page 234 for instructions.)

2. Using the strands of vine, make a small 7-inch-diameter wreath for the lid and a 4-inch high oval for the handle.

3. For the spout, twist several vines together to form a solid 9-inch-long piece and bend it to form the spout.

4. Cut small pieces of spool wire and tie the handle, lid, and spout onto the large oval to complete the teapot.

5. Turn the teapot to the "wrong" side and run hot glue all around the pot. Press on a whole piece of sheet moss, green side down. Repeat for the lid.

6. Turn the pot right side up and trim any excess moss. Glue on dried flowers for decoration.

## What You Do for the Urn

1. In addition to the materials listed on page 224, you will need one stick, the thickness of a pencil and equal in length to the diameter of the wreath.

2. Twist six to eight 20-inch-long strands of vine into a bundle. Tie it 4 inches from each end with spool wire.

3. Take the stick and tie it horizontally to one end of the vine bundle with spool wire. Bring the other end of the bundle up to form a U and tie it to the stick.

4. Add two strands of vine for the handles, tying them on with pieces of wire.

5. Make a small fan of 4-inch-long pieces of vine and tie together with wire. Wire the fan to the bottom of the urn.

6. Turn the urn to the "wrong" side and run hot glue all around the body of the urn. Press on a whole piece of sheet moss, green side down.

7. Turn the urn right side up and trim any excess moss. Then either glue on flowers or wire a bunch of flowers to the cross-stick in the back.

## What You Do for the Bell

1. Twist six to eight 24-inch-long strands of vine into a bundle. Tie the bundle 4 inches from each end with a piece of spool wire. This is the base of the bell, as shown in the photo on page 225.

2. Twist ten to twelve 32-inch-long strands of vine into a bundle. Tie the bundle 4 inches from one end. Then wire it to one end of the base bundle so that the bundles are perpendicular to each other.

3. To form the bell, bend the 32-inch-long bundle down to meet the other end of the base bundle. Attach it to the base with wire.

4. Make a 3-inch-diameter wreath and tie it to the top of the bell for the handle. (See "Woven Vine" or "Wrapped Vine" on page 234 for instructions.) Use a flower for the clapper or make another small wreath and wire it on.

5. Turn the bell to the "wrong" side and run hot glue all around the body of the bell. Press on a whole piece of sheet moss, green side down.

6. Turn the bell right side up and trim any excess moss. Decorate the bell with dried flowers and leaves.

## What You Do for the Pineapple

1. In addition to the wreath materials listed on page 224, you will need about 35 long, thin, dried leaves, like palm fronds.

2. Using the strands of pliable vine, make a 13-inch-high oval wreath base. (See "Woven Vine" or "Wrapped Vine" on page 234 for instructions.) Press the top of the sides in toward the center to narrow the top of the wreath, forming a pineapple shape.

## WREATHMAKER'S ❧WISDOM❦

*Pick vines during the growing season (from spring to fall in the North). If you pick vines in the winter, you must immerse them in a tub of hot water for 12 to 24 hours, until they become pliable.*

*If your sheet moss is in separate pieces rather than one whole piece, cut corrugated cardboard to fit and glue to the back of the wreath. Then glue the sheet moss to the front of the cardboard and continue decorating.*

2. Using the strands of pliable vine, make a 16-inch-high oval wreath base. (See "Woven Vine" or "Wrapped Vine" on page 234 for instructions.) To narrow the wreath at the neck end, tightly wire across one end with spool wire, binding the two sides together until the vines are dry; the wires will be removed later.

3. Using the 28-inch-long wrapped vine to make the head and neck, bind one end of the wrapped vine to the narrow end of the wreath. Now draw down the head to make a pleasing curve. Bind the head and the neck together with spool wire to hold the curve until the vines dry.

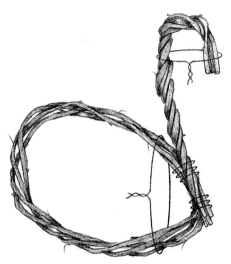

3. Turn the pineapple to the "wrong" side and run hot glue all around the body of the pineapple. Press on a whole piece of sheet moss, green side down. Glue a fan of leaves to the top back.

4. Turn the pineapple right side up and trim off any excess moss. Then glue on dried flowers to decorate the front of the pineapple, as desired.

## What You Do for the Swan

1. In addition to the wreath materials listed on page 224, you will need one cluster of tightly wrapped vine (about 28 inches long) and long, thin, dried leaves, like palm fronds.

4. When the vines are dry in several weeks, cut the wires. Turn the swan to the "wrong" side and run hot glue all around the body. Press on a whole piece of sheet moss, green side down. Enlarge the head with more moss or flowers, if desired.

5. Turn the swan right side up and trim the excess moss. Using the long leaves, add tail feathers and then dried flowers for decoration, as desired.

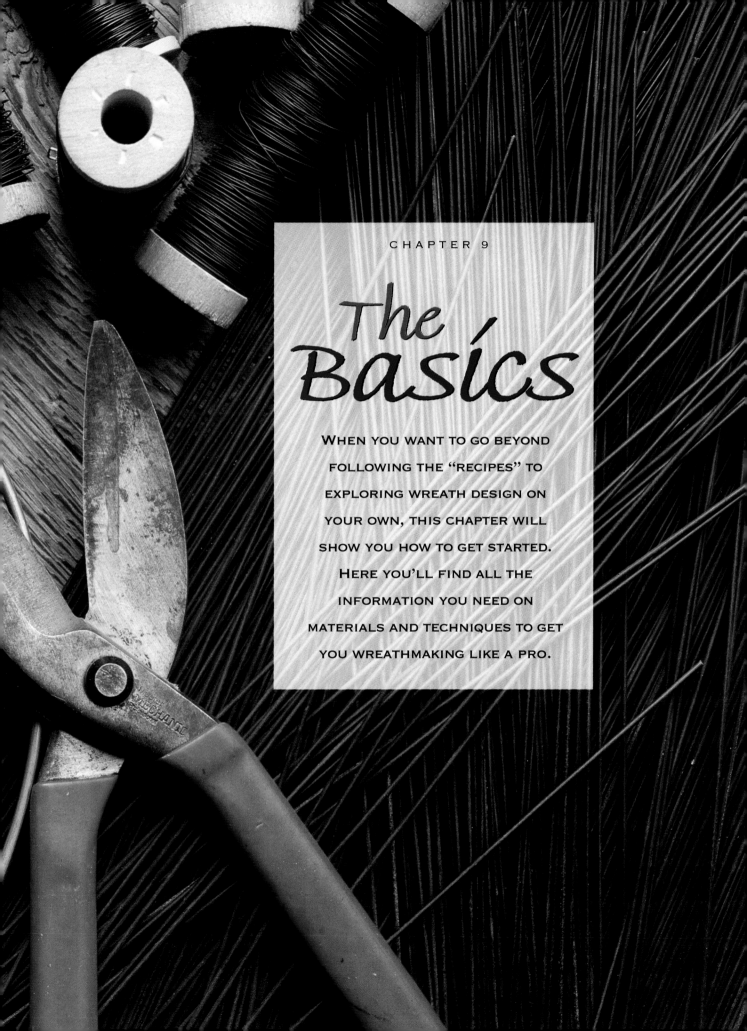

CHAPTER 9

# The Basics

When you want to go beyond following the "recipes" to exploring wreath design on your own, this chapter will show you how to get started. Here you'll find all the information you need on materials and techniques to get you wreathmaking like a pro.

# Design Your Own Wreath

Just because you start with a purchased wreath base doesn't mean that you can't end with a design of your own. I began with six identical 24-inch-diameter sweet huckleberry wreath bases and created six distinct styles by emphasizing different aspects of the wreath.

## Swirl Wreath

This wreath (*bottom left*) emphasizes the swirled lines of the twigs. Hot-glue flowers between the twigs using only material that grows along the stem, like larkspur, rat-tail statice, and green amaranth. The fuller this wreath is with flowers, the prettier it is.

## Wrapped Wreath

You can change the very shape of this wreath (*bottom right*) by tightly wrapping two-thirds of the base with narrow ribbon. Tie ribbon to the back of the base at both ends. Now decorate the other third with dried materials and glue some additional ribbon among the flowers. By wrapping different amounts of the wreath, you can vary the entire look. This wreath looks much smaller than the others though it was the same size to start.

## Flower-Covered Wreath

Very little of the huckleberry shows through this millefleur-designed wreath (*top center*). The more flowers you use, the more excitement you create. Cut stems very short and glue all material directly to the twigs.

## Center Arrangement

When you look at a doughnut, do you see the doughnut or the hole? When you are designing wreaths, think of the branches, the tips, or the center. Concentrate your design in a particular area, and you will conjure up an idea for something different. To make an arrangement in the center of a wreath, cut out a circle of corrugated cardboard and glue it to the back of the wreath base. Glue a thin layer of brown floral foam to the cardboard and use it to hold the stems of the dried materials. In the wreath here (*bottom center*), the hydrangea tumbles out of the center well, and the wreath itself seems to recede in the background. This design makes an unusual centerpiece.

## Wreath with Swag

Continue the thought of the wreath as a background or frame. Make a swag of dried materials at least 30 inches long. In this wreath (*top right*), I've used birch branches, 'Silver King' artemisia, and cockscomb. Bundle the materials and wrap them tightly together in the center with floral spool wire. Use more wire to tie the swag to the wreath. Placing the swag vertically through the center of the wreath, horizontally across the bottom, or horizontally across the top changes the appearance of the overall design.

## Three-Part Wreath

Make three small bows and glue them to the wreath at the two, six, and ten o'clock positions, as I did here (*top left*). Cluster all the dried materials around these bows and glue them to the twigs. The use of three small bows rather than the usual large one changes the look of the wreath.

# How to Make Your Own Wreath Base

Give any wreath a custom look by changing its size or shape to fit your decorating needs. Make your own base or modify one that you buy in one of the ways suggested here.

## Woven Vine

Make this style in any size and with any fresh or pliable vine. If your vines are not fresh, immerse them in a tub of hot water for 12 to 24 hours so they become supple enough to work with them.

Here's how to make a round or oval wreath base with an all-natural look using no wire. How much vine you use depends on the diameter of the wreath and the thickness desired.

1. Strip the leaves off the strands of vine. With one hand, hold the longest strand at the thicker end. With your other hand, bend down the opposite end of the vine to form a circle that is slightly smaller than the desired diameter of the finished wreath.

2. Weave the remainder of the strand in and out along the circle you have formed, as shown in the illustration. When you are finished, the circle should hold by itself.

3. Take another long strand of vine and weave it in and out along the circle until you have used up that piece. Each time you start a new strand of vine, place the thick end along the weakest part of the wreath. Continue weaving until you have reached the desired thickness.

## Wrapped Vine

Select fresh or pliable vines. This wreath is wrapped either with floral spool wire or a thick, flexible strand of vine, or both. It is often less wild looking than the woven wreath on the left.

1. Strip the leaves off the strands of vine. Select a long, strong, pliable strand and set it aside. Take the longest remaining strand and form a circle of the desired diameter, following the directions in Step 1 under "Woven Vine." Keep wrapping the vine around the circle until it is all used up. Use small pieces of wire to tie the circle together if necessary.

2. Take the next strand of vine and add it to the circle. Keep adding vine around the circle, all the while holding it with one hand.

3. Wrap spool wire around the circle to hold it together. If desired, wrap the reserved strand of vine over the spool wire to hide the wire.

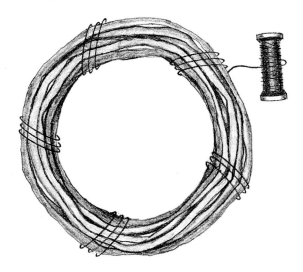

## Single-Wire Frame

Am I the only one in the world who hates wire coat hangers for making wreath bases? How come I can't bend the hanger wire into a nice, neat circle?

Instead I start with wire, like 14- or 16-gauge, from the hardware store. The smaller the finished wreath, the thinner the wire can be. The finished wreath will be airy and delicate. You can vary the size and the shape—forming a square, rectangle, diamond, heart, or almost any shape you want.

1. Gather your materials. You'll need wire for the frame, wire cutters, floral tape, floral spool wire, and plant material for decoration.

2. Form the size and shape base you want, leaving 6 to 8 extra inches on each end. Cut the wire. Form a loop at each end of the wire and hook together.

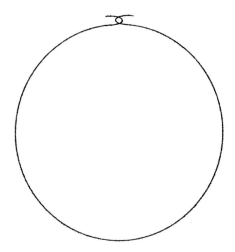

3. Wrap the whole wreath base with floral tape, completely covering the wire.

4. Tie the spool wire to the frame. Place a small bundle of plant material against the frame and wrap with the spool wire. Continue adding bundles and wrapping until you have gone all around the wreath. Tie off and cut the spool wire.

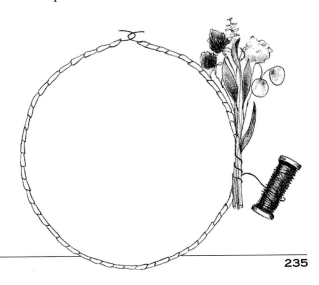

# Working with Purchased Wreath Bases

There are four types of wreath bases that I use quite often—straw bases, wire wreath frames with clamps, wire box frames, and foam bases. Here are my techniques for working with each of them.

## Straw Wreath Base

I always purchase my straw wreath bases. They are inexpensive and come in a wide variety of shapes and sizes. And because they are pressed together by a machine, they are far more compact and sturdy than anything I could make.

1. Gather your materials. You'll need floral pins, the straw base, and plant material for decoration.

2. Make a bundle with six to ten stems of plant material. Lay it on the straw base, slanting outward, and pin it in place. Push the floral pin in at an angle rather than straight down. Take the next bundle of stems and pin it directly on top of the wreath. Pin a third

bundle directly on top of the other two, slightly angling it in toward the center. Continue around the straw base in this way, alternating the direction of the bundles as you pin them until you have covered the base.

3. Then go back to where you started and lay another bundle over the stems of the first, hiding the ends. Usually I work up to three tiers, but this depends entirely on the thickness and type of material. Just be sure to use enough material to conceal the stems, pins, and as much of the straw base as you want to hide while making the wreath as full as you want it to be. Don't be stingy with the floral pins. It's better to use smaller bundles of material and more pins than to risk the pins popping out from being overstuffed.

## Wire Wreath Frame with Clamps

This frame is complete in itself and ready to accept your materials. It is reusable, and the clamps, once closed, are easily reopened to make necessary changes.

1. Gather your materials. You'll need the wreath frame and plant material for decoration. Count the number of clamps on the frame. A 10-inch-diameter frame usually has 10 clamps; a 14-inch-diameter frame has 14 clamps. In

selecting the size frame to work with, remember that your materials will greatly enlarge the finished design. For example, a 14-inch-diameter wreath frame can be used to make a 40-inch-diameter evergreen wreath. It can also be used to make a smaller wreath.

2. Divide your plant materials into even piles—one pile for each clamp. Set the stems of one pile into one of the wire clamps. Bend the wires over the stems tightly, one side at a time.

3. Take the next pile and lay it in the clamp below the first pile, overlapping and hiding the previous stems. Clamp it in place.

4. Continue around the frame in this manner. To make sure the material is very tight and won't slip out, turn the wreath over and insert unused pieces of stems into any spaces in the clamps. There's always room for extra pieces, and they won't show from the front.

## Wire Box Frame

This type of wire frame is great for holding evergreens and cones. They fit snugly when pushed in from behind. Then turn the frame over to complete your decorating. If you cover a wire box frame, it makes an attractive base for dried materials. Use green sheet moss or Spanish moss for different effects.

1. Gather your materials. You'll need the wreath frame, floral spool wire, green sheet moss or Spanish moss, and plant materials for decoration.

2. Lay the moss over the front and sides of the box frame. Tie the end of floral spool wire to the frame. Wrap the wire around the frame to hold the moss in place. Tie off and cut the wire.

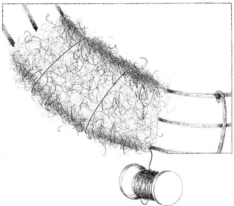

3. Make a bundle with six to ten stems of plant material. Attach the materials to the moss-covered frame by wrapping on with spool wire. (See "Single-Wire Frame" on page 235 for details.)

## Extruded Foam Wreath Base

This wreath base has reinforced wire, making it suitable for very large or very heavy wreaths. It can also be painted, as I did for "A Wreath in the Style of Josiah Wedgwood," shown on page 16. To attach materials to this base, simply wrap them on. (See "Single-Wire Frame" on page 235.)

# Give Tired Wreaths a Face-Lift

Water and sun will turn plant material from dried to dead in a few short months. This wreath (*inset photo*) hung on a barn door beneath a small overhang from May through September when I deemed it ready for the compost heap. Exposed to summer humidity, blowing rain and wind, and strong sunlight, the colors faded to nothingness. The bedraggled ribbon was once melon-colored. A similar wreath without the bow is pictured in its original splendor at the top left of the photo shown on page 179.

Refurbish any vine wreath in short order by stripping off all the old decoration. With a hot glue gun handy and a ribbon that fits the season, create an entirely different look. Here, the spring wreath (*bottom right*) uses pastels and white as the defining colors; the summer wreath (*bottom left*) features roses; and the fall wreath (*top left*) exhibits a range of golds and oranges typical of a Pennsylvania autumn. For winter, silver spray paint transforms the vine (*top right*). Flowers and pods get the same treatment. Once the wreath is sprayed silver, you can't turn it back to natural; but for another spring, paint over it with pale blue enamel.

# caring for your wreaths

Some wreaths you create are meant to be ephemeral. You make them for a special season, an important event, or a party, and you don't really care how long they last. The "Welcoming the Bride" wreath on page 98 is one such design. Keep fresh wreaths away from direct sunlight and drafts when possible. Mist with water frequently when your "absolutely necessary" location is less than ideal for the flowers; and remember to water according to the directions for making the wreaths.

When you invest time, money, and creative effort, you want your wreath to last as long as possible. Proper placement is a key to longevity. Dried materials should be protected from moisture and sunlight to retard fading and from wind to prevent overall destruction. Some materials are more fragile than others. Choose sturdy statice, strawflowers, and other everlastings over the more delicate larkspur and hydrangea for a front door. Select a door that

doesn't get constant banging from throngs of people brushing by or from kids running in and out. For those difficult sites, select tough vine, decorative ribbon, and the most rigid construction methods. Hang your more delicate wreaths indoors where they will be highly visible but away from the main traffic pattern. And for those of you who have indoor cats, inquisitive dogs, and prying toddler's fingers, a decorative wreath hung nice and high is the key to your dried-flower protection program.

Please note: We photographed a few of the wreaths in this book in outdoor settings that make luscious photos but are not ideal for the long life of the wreath. Definitely do as I say and not as I (sometimes) show.

Store out-of-season dried wreaths in an airtight black garbage bag to which you have added some mothballs or insect repellent. Keep the bag where it won't be disturbed, and you'll have pristine wreaths to use year after year.

# Making a Bow

Many crafters are nervous about bow making, but you needn't be. Here are some steps to making a perfect bow. These instructions are for an average-size door wreath, 18 to 25 inches in diameter. You'll need 2 to 3 yards of ribbon, a 6-inch-long thin piece of wire, and scissors. Note that these instructions are for ribbon with no "wrong" side.

1. Hold the ribbon between your thumb and fingers, about 11 inches from one end. Make a 4-inch loop and hold it under your thumb.

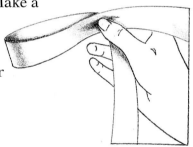

2. Make another 4-inch loop in the opposite direction and hold it under your thumb.

3. Continue forming additional pairs of loops to the left and right, each time making the pairs about ½ inch smaller. You will have enough ribbon to make two to four pairs of loops, depending on the width of the ribbon and the proportions you want. If you are using ribbon with a right and a wrong side, follow the same instructions, but each time you bring the loop to the center, twist the ribbon so the right side will be up on the next loop.

4. Still holding the bow under your thumb, make a 1-inch loop in the center. Let the tail come down behind this small loop.

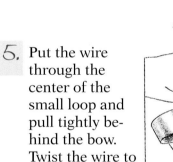

5. Put the wire through the center of the small loop and pull tightly behind the bow. Twist the wire to secure all the loops.

6. Trim the ribbon ends on a slant with sharp scissors. Use extra wire to attach the bow to your project.

*NOTE: You can make a raffia bow by piling up several strands of raffia and, treating them like one ribbon, tie a simple bow (just like you tie your shoelaces).*

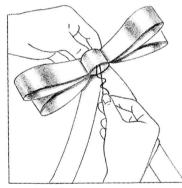

# WREATHMAKING NECESSITIES

*There are some items that no serious wreathmaker should be
without. Here's what I recommend and use most often.*

| MATERIALS | DESCRIPTIONS AND USES |
|---|---|
| Clippers | Use to cut thick or woody stems. A wide variety is available. |
| Floral cage | Floral foam encased in a plastic cage. It comes in various sizes. There are holes near the base of the cage so you can easily wire it onto a wreath. |
| Floral clay | Comes in a roll protected by paper on one side. It has the consistency of chewing gum. To use, tear off about 1 inch, remove the paper, and stretch out the clay. Press the clay on any dry, clean surface you want to adhere. |
| Floral foam | For fresh flowers use green bricks, which absorb water. Before using, soak the foam in a bucket of water for 30 minutes until saturated. Never reuse foam that has held fresh flowers; it could harbor destructive bacteria. |
| | For dried flowers use brown bricks, which are nonabsorbent. They come in hard extruded foam (like Styrofoam) for thick stems and branches, or softer foam for delicate stems. Cut the foam with a paring knife to suit your needs. |
| Floral pick | Use to attach plant material to a wreath or to lengthen or strengthen stems. You can shorten the pick by cutting a new point with clippers. |
| | To use, take a small bunch of stems and lay the bottom 2 inches of stem along the top 2 inches of the pick. Wrap the wire around the stems, then secure with a layer of floral tape. |
| Floral pin | Use to attach material to straw wreath bases. The most versatile are 1¾ inches long. |
| Floral preservative | Also called fresh-flower food. It prevents bacterial growth, which shortens the life of the flowers. Use a powdered commercial product or mix three drops of liquid bleach per pint of water. |
| Floral prong | Use to secure wet or dry foam to a container. Put a layer of floral clay on the bottom of the prong and press it down onto the container. Place floral foam over the prong. |
| Floral tape | Comes in brown, green, white, and other colors. To use, gently pull out a length of tape to stretch it. Wrap a stem by overlapping the tape as you twist it around the stem. |
| Floral water pick | A plastic tube with a point on the bottom and a rubber cap with a hole. Fill with water and slip the stem of a well-conditioned fresh flower through the hole. Add water as necessary. The pointed end can stand in floral foam. |
| Glue, craft | Useful in place of hot glue on metal and where there will be a wide fluctuation in temperatures. It doesn't harden as quickly as hot glue; wait for it to set before continuing your project. |

| MATERIALS | DESCRIPTIONS AND USES |
|---|---|
| Glue, spray adhesive | Available in art supply stores. It's useful for paper projects. |
| Glue gun | Comes in hot and low-temperature versions, or ones that switch from hot to low-temperature. I prefer hot glue for most craft work (but hot glue doesn't work with metal). Get a gun with a self-advancing glue stick. Keep fingers away from dribbling glue. Keep a cup of cold water handy to dunk fingers that get glue on them. Low-temperature glue will not burn your fingers, and it sets faster than hot glue but isn't quite as strong. |
| Knife, utility | Use to cut and score corrugated cardboard. |
| Oasis foam ring | A brand of floral foam ring that has a plastic coating on the bottom. It absorbs water and is used for fresh floral projects. |
| Protective spray | Use to protect materials from bugs and humidity. For dried fruits, breads, and vegetables, use polyurethane, shellac, or varnish in matte or glossy finish. Spray several coats on all sides of the items.<br><br>For flowers that have been dried in silica gel, use a surface sealer. Spray them with at least three light coats, allowing each coat to dry before respraying. |
| Ribbon, paper | Comes in rolls, either twisted or untwisted. To untwist, soak the ribbon in water for five minutes. Wring out the water, gently untwist the ribbon, and hang over a shower curtain rod to dry. |
| Ribbon, wire-edged | Has an extremely thin wire running down both sides of the ribbon. It makes an expert bow maker out of everyone because the wire holds the loops and tails wherever they're wanted. |
| Silica gel | An excellent desiccant for drying roses and orchids. It has the appearance and consistency of white sugar. Always use a dust mask when working with it to prevent breathing in the powder. Every package comes with directions. |
| Wire, chicken | Comes in different widths and coatings at hardware and floral supply stores. It's useful for making frames for wreaths and topiaries and to stuff in the neck of vases to hold an arrangement in place. |
| Wire, floral (stub) | Comes precut in different gauges (widths). Buy 16- to 18-gauge for thicker wire, 22- to 24-gauge for thinner wire. "Bright" stub wire looks silvery when new, darkens over time, and rusts when wet. It's ideal to use when wiring strawflowers or globe amaranths. |
| Wire, floral spool | Green-coated and comes in different gauges (widths). Higher numbers indicate thinner widths. Use 22- or 24-gauge for wrapping materials to wreath frames. |
| Wire cutters | Use for all your floral needs. Save your good clippers and scissors by using wire cutters. |

# Acknowledgments

My utmost gratitude to the friends and neighbors who allowed us to invade their homes and gardens to photograph the "ultimate" wreaths.

- The Evan Bowen Sr. House, Orwigsburg, Pa.
- Catherine Ann and Dennis Degler
- Dot and Dennis Dunn
- Ellen and Ernie Fink
- Toni and Max Groff
- Hidden Treasures, McKeansburg, Pa.
- Lorraine and Don Jones
- Laura Kauffman
- Sharon and Jay Linard
- Jack and Mary Miller
- Ellen Plano and Donald Brown
- Barbara Pressler
- Danielle and John Richards
- Susan L. M. Smith
- Miriam Wintersteen

These kind people lent the perfect props and plant materials just when I was most desperate.

- Dolores Delin
- Marie Fisher
- Rugh Ling
- Simon Maurer
- Rebecca's Restaurant, Orwigsburg, Pa.
- Barbara Shaw
- Joan Steel
- Stonehedge, Tamaqua, Pa.
- Teddy Bears & Us, Orwigsburg, Pa.
- Anna Wentz

Special thanks to Art Reinke of Loose Ends Paper Company of Keizer, Oregon (503-390-7457) for the project papers and paper ribbon.

# Suggested Reading

Dawson, Aileen. *Masterpieces of Wedgwood in the British Museum.* London: British Museum Publications Ltd., 1984.

Platt, Ellen Spector. *Flower Crafts: A Step-by-Step Guide to Growing, Drying and Decorating with Flowers.* Emmaus, Pa.: Rodale Press, 1993.

———. *Wreaths, Arrangements and Basket Decorations: Using Flowers, Foliage, Herbs and Grasses to Make Colorful Crafts.* Emmaus, Pa.: Rodale Press, 1994.

Rountree, Susan Hight. *Christmas Decorations from Williamsburg.* Williamsburg, Va.: The Colonial Williamsburg Foundation, 1992.

# Seed Sources

The companies listed here have catalogs filled with flowers, grasses, and pods to dry. Read the fine print for other suggestions and look at the planting information for sun and water requirements, hardiness zones, and so forth.

Bountiful Gardens
18001 Shafer Ranch Road
Willits, CA 95490
(707) 459-6410

W. Atlee Burpee & Co.
300 Park Avenue
Warminster, PA 18991
(800) 333-5808

The Cook's Garden
P.O. Box 535
Londonderry, VT 05148
(802) 824-3400

Henry Field's Seed & Nursery Co.
415 N. Burnett Street
Shenandoah, IA 51602
(605) 665-4491

Harris Seeds
P.O. Box 22960
60 Saginaw Drive
Rochester, NY 14692
(800) 544-7938

Johnny's Selected Seeds
Foss Hill Road
Albion, ME 04910
(207) 437-4357

Nichols Garden Nursery
1190 N. Pacific Highway
Albany, OR 97321
(503) 928-9280

Park Seed Co.
Cokesbury Road
Greenwood, SC 29647
(800) 845-3369

Shepherd's Garden Seeds
30 Irene Street
Torrington, CT 06790
(203) 482-3638

Thompson & Morgan, Inc.
P.O. Box 1308
Jackson, NJ 08527
(800) 274-7333